THE TAMILIAN ANTIQUARY

EDITOR

PANDIT D. SAVARIROYAN

VOL. I NO. 1-10: VOL. II. NO. 1-2

VOL. I. NO. 4

THE TAMILIAN ANTIQUARY

EDITOR

PANDIT D. SAVARIROYAN

VOL. I NO. 1-10: VOL. II. NO. 1-2

VOL. I. NO. 4

MANIKKA VACAGAR
AND
HIS DATE

K.G. SESHA AIYAR

MANIKKA VACAGAR
AND THE
EARLY CHRISTIANS OF MALABAR

T. PONNAMBALAM PILLAI

Published by

Gyan Publishing House
5, Ansari Road
Daryaganj, New Delhi-110002
Phone: 011-47034999, 9811692060
E-mail: books@gyanbooks.com

Distribution Network
gyanbooks.com
India, USA, Canada, UK, Australia, France

ISBN : 978-81-212-3057-5 (PB)
First Published, Trichinopoly, 1909

2nd Impression 2020

Printed at: Gyan Press, Delhi.

MANIKKA VACAGAR

AND

HIS DATE.

BY

K. G. SESHA AIYAR, Esq., B.A., B.L., M.R.A.S.,

HIGH COURT VAKIL, TRIVANDRAM.

CONTENTS.

Manikka Vaçagar

AND

HIS DATE.

I. The spiritual value of the Tiru Vaçagam.

தேசகத்தி லினிக்கின்ற தெள்ளமுதே மாணிக்க
வாசகனே யானந்த வடிவான மாதவனே
மாசகன்ற நீதிருவாய் மலர்ந்ததமிழ் மாமறையி
னாசகன்ற வனுபவநா னநுபவிக்க வருளுதியே.

வான்கலந்த மாணிக்க வாசகநின் வாசகத்தை
நான்கலந்து பாடுங்கா னற்கருப்பஞ் சாற்றினிலே
தேன்கலந்து பால்கலந்து செழுங்கனித்தீஞ் சுவைகலந்தென்
னூன்கலந்து வுயிர்கலந்து வுவட்டாம லினிப்பதுவே.

வாட்டமிலா மாணிக்க வாசகநின் வாசகத்தைக்
கேட்டபொழு தங்கிருந்த கீழ்ப்பறவைச் சாதிகளும்
வேட்டமுறும் பொல்லாவி லங்குகளு மெய்ஞ்ஞானம்
நாட்டமுறு மென்னிலிங்கு நானடைதல் வியப்பன்றே.

Ramalinga Swamigal's Arul-pa.

"Love great men ; love, venerate and bow down in submission before them. Does not every true man feel that he is himself made higher by doing reverence to what is really above him ?" These words of Carlyle come to my mind when I think of the sage that sang the supremely beautiful lyrics of the *Tiru Vaçagam*. Manikka Vaçagar is among the greatest of our saints who renounced the pomp and pageantry of the world to walk humbly with God. No work is held in higher estimation and veneration by the Tamils than Manikka Vacagar's "Sacred Song". There are few poems in Tamil devotional literature that can compare with the *Tiru Vacagam* in light and sweetness, in grace and earnestness, in lofty feeling and fervid piety, in passionate longing for spiritual peace and purity and in the uplifting faith in divine grace in which the human soul, tossed about on the stormy billows of intellectual and moral puzzles, finds a safe haven of rest. The music of Manikka Vacagar's melting lyrics and their glowing faith and fervour have for centuries continued to thrill with rapturous emotion the teeming millions of the Tamil country whose story of spiritual growth, of spiritual struggle and spiritual triumph, has been permanently influenced by them. To the Tamils, Manikka Vacagar has always been 'the saint whose words are sweetest honey,' capable of quenching the thirst of their yearning souls. or whose utterances are 'precious rubies,' forming a treasure-house full of accents of the Holy Ghost. The song of hope and love and redeeming grace is a rich heritage to humanity in whatever language it may be written; and let us hope that the late Dr. Pope's great translation, in which we find a marvellous reflection of the sublime beauty, the intense piety, the sincere personal devotion and the irresistible fervour of spirit that breathe through Manikka-Vacagar's lyrics, will help the West to appreciate and realize the spirituality, the living faith and devotion that exist in our daily life.

The central incident of Manikka-Vacagar's life is his sudden conversion to the service of God, while he was in the prime of youth and in the plenitude of temporal power. He is commissioned by his sovereign Arimartana Pandya to proceed to Tiru-perun-turai to purchase horses, and there the conversion takes place. As the royal cavalcade, with the youthful prime-minister at the head, draws near the town, the chant of the sacred Caiva Agamas rises in solemn mysterious strains from a neighbouring grove, and the youth reverently alights and approaches the spot whence the mystic music proceeds. From that instant his secular life is over. He beholds with rapture a mystic Guru seated at the foot of a spreading "*Kurunthu*" (*Atalantia Missionis*) bedecked with rosaries of scarlet eleocarpus beads, smeared with holy ashes, and surrounded by an admiring and intently listening host of disciples. The crisis has come and the youthful minister of state becomes a *Jivanmukta.* He is initiated, and is from that moment "one in feeling, soul, power and faculty with the Infinite Eternal". He exchanges his rich garments and adornments for the habiliments of the ascetic and the holy ashes. He wakes,

> From the dream, the probation, the prelude, to find himself set
> Clear and safe in new light and new life.

For it is a fundamental doctrine of the Caiva Siddhanta that the present life is a probation, a period of preparation for ultimate communion and fellowship with the Supreme. Our life and our suffering is a gracious appointment of Civa for the salvation of the human soul.

> Put pain from out the world, what room were left,
> For thanks to God, for love to man?

And the instrument of release from all embodiment is that wisdom which understands the Divine purpose and adapts itself to it. Realizing this, the young sage for ever renounces the world and in the consciousness of Primal Love which

> Fills infinitude wholly, nor leaves up nor down
> One spot for the creature to stand in.

he seeks his reward and repose in the God-head:

> Transcendent One, extending through both earth and heaven,
> Thou see'st to none but Thee I cling!
> O Civa-puram's King! In glorious beauty bright,
> Civan, in holy Perunturai's shrine
> Who dwell'st! To whom make I my plaint, whom blame, if Thou
> Who mads't me Thine deny Thy grace?
> Thou see'st no joy have I upon this sea-girt earth;
> Be gracious, bid me come to thee!— Hymn XXVIII, Verse I.

In Perun-turrai girt with ordered stately groves,
'neath the Kurunthan's flow'ry shade,
I call to mind Thy glories all, and pondering yearn,
and as my mighty Lord Thee oft invoke.
Ascetic rare! When I, Thy servant, craving call,
struggling amid the billowy sea,
In grace declare the fitting path to reach
the silver hill and *bid me come* !—

Hymn XXIX, Verse X.

In almost every one of the hymns of the *Tiru-Vacagam* he alludes to this crisis in his life, and pours forth in ecstasy his thanks-giving for the redeeming grace of Civa, whose humble slave he has become.

Thou only one, to Whom can none compare! Thou Light
shining within the very soul of me, Thy slave!
On me who knew not the true goal,—of merit void,—
O Love unique!—Thou hast choice grace bestowed.
O radiant Form Whose splendour bright no tongue can tell!
My Wealth of bliss! O Civa Peruman!
In weariness—I've seized Thee—hold Thee fast! Henceforth,
Ah, whither grace imparting would'st Thou rise?

Hymn XXXVII, Verse V.

With the mendicant's staff and the mendicant's bowl, he goes forth singing in melodious strains rich with the nectar of sacred and devout poetry, the glory and love of his Divine Master.

The potsherd and the skull I deemed my kin : my soul dissolved;
Wealth to be sought was Civan's foot alone, I clearly saw;
With soul and body to the earth in worship bent, a slave,
I 've reached him where he dances, Lord of Tillai's home of joy !

Hymn XL, Verse I.

I lay as one who tills a barren field and reaps no crop;—
'Twas then the gain of penance done of old accrued; and thus
Before the Caivan's roseate lotus foot I bent my worthless head
His own,—I 've reached Him Who bears rule in Tillai's home of joy!

Hymn XL, Verse IX.

He marches steadfastly heavenward, despising all earthly allurements, and perfectly resigned to the will of Civa.

That very day my soul, my body, all to me
    Pertaining, didst Thou not take as Thy own,
Thou like a mountain strong! when me Thou mad'st Thy slave?
    And this day is there any hindrance found in me?
Our mighty One! Eight-armed and triple-eyed!
    Do Thou to me what 's good alone, or do Thou ill,
To all resigned, I 'm Thine and wholly Thine!

Hymn XXXIII, Verse VII.

But a spirit of resignation to the Divine will is not inconsistent with a supplication for grace and mercy and release from the bondage of life. Indeed Manikka-Vacagar was a great believer in the efficacy of prayer and of humble worship paid to the Deity who, in the conception of the sage, is 'all-abounding Love,' 'the vast ambrosial Sea of grace;' and hence such passionate appeals as the following are very frequent in the *Tiru-vacagam;*—

The tongue itself that cries to Thee—all other powers
    of my whole being that cry out,—all are Thyself!
Thou art my way of strength! The trembling thrill that runs
    through me is Thee! Thyself the whole of ill and weal!
None other here! Would one unfold and truly utter Thee
    what way to apprehend? Thou, Lord of Civa-world!
And if I trembling fear, should'st Thou not comfort me?

Hymn XXXIII, Verse V.

The hymns of the *Tiru-Vacagam* are a record of our sage's struggles against the ways of the flesh which, we find, once filled him almost with despair, and of his ultimate triumph over sin through his abiding faith in Civa's boundless grace. The young soul finding no relief in ceremonial acts cries for light to the Master who has apparently deserted it, but gradually derives strength and sustenance from its unshaken confidence in immortal Love. Nothing can be more inspiring than the transition from the early 'spirit of heaviness' to the buoyancy of hope and the certitude of Divine grace which characterize the later poems. While tossed by the broad billows of anguish on the 'Sea of birth,' the sage tells us that he thought and ultimately seized 'the raft of the Five Letters,' which showed him 'a boundless fertile shore' and made him, till then "the rash insensate one," God's own.

It is the Caiva Siddhanta that generated in Manikka-Vacagar his self-negating love for his Divine Master, and impelled him to cry in ecstasy—

> Glory I ask not; nor desire I wealth; not earth or heaven I crave;
> I seek nor birth nor death; those that desire not Civan never more
> I touch. I have reached the foot of sacred Perunturai's king,
> And crown'd myself! I go not forth! I know no going hence again!
>
> Hymn XXXIV, Verse VII.

and seek through the grace of Civa divine wisdom, that he might live eternally in the full and conscious enjoyment of his Father's presence, in conclusive bliss, finally emancipated from embodiment and redeemed from sin.

> The God of Gods, to king of Gods unknown;
> King of the three, what teeming worlds create,
> Preserve, destroy; the First; Essence divine;
> The Sire of Sires, Father, whose half the mother is;
> The King of all! He came, and made me, too, His own.
> Henceforth I 'm no one's vassal; none I fear!
> I 've reached the goal; with servants of His saints
> In sea of bliss I evermore shall bathe!
>
> Hymn V, Verse XXX.

That was what Manikka-Vacagar strove for and attained and in his songs the mission of his life to his countrymen is enshrined. The hymns of the *Tiru-vacagam* are songs of faith and love and grace and immortality, of spiritual struggle and spiritual triumph—themes that are of the highest significance to all mankind; and who, on reading them, will fail to realise how in every age and race, under varying conditions of organisation and development, are found the same essential insights, tendencies, aspirations and demands? Perhaps our Western friends will, on persuing the lyrics, feel that there is in us a strange combination of high spirituality and gross idolatory. That is the feeling of even Dr. Pope who has spent a whole lifetime in understanding and appreciating the thoughts and feelings of the Tamil people regarding the highest matters, their conception and solution of the great problems of God, the soul, humanity, nature, evil, suffering and the unseen world. As for our so-called idolatory, we should really be pardoned if we refuse to belive that our symbology has been as well understood by the West as it deserves to be. The precise import of our symbolical expressions may not so naturally become patent to people in the West as to us; and for this the settled convictions of ages that the East and the West havo each inherited, are mainly responsible. Some of the sublimest ideas which the West regards as emphatically beyond the sphere of argument and of the cold intellect, the orthodox Hindu fails to appreciate however much he may have been influenced by Western philosophy and culture; even as Dr. Pope, with all his love and sympathy for the Caivas and their cherished convictions, finds it not altogether easy to realise in the symbol of Nataraja an object to inspire and elevate. The Hindu realizes in Nataraja the idea of the true Guru or preceptor who teaches that *maya* or illusion should be suppressed, that the world should become subject to us and not we to the world, that the *Atman* is far beyond the reach of the mind that is swayed by fleeting desires, that *Ahankara* should be destroyed and that man should strive to elevate himself to the region of pure unconditioned consciousness, free from passion and deception, and to deserve the equability, the bliss, the light and the truth that really form the self. The foreigner thinks all this is fanciful; we, however, hold it as a living faith. But we must have our differences, for otherwise thought would cease. Nevertheless both the East and the West, however different the symbols of their religious systems may be, must be prepared to recognize, as Dr. Pope earnestly pleads they should, that every system has its truths and profounder thoughts; and these lie deeper than 'full fathoms five' in man's nature; and must be fundamentally and essentially in large measure the same for all men and for all time. Cudworth, the English Platonist, wrote: 'If that were true which is commonly taken for granted, that the generality of tho Pagan nations acknowledged no sovereign numen, but scattered their devotion amongst a multitude of independent deities, this would have much stumbled the naturality of the Divine idea': an effect that to his large and clear mind was equivalent to disproval of the divineness itself. The study of comparative religion will show us that the cardinal virtues and moral earnestness belong to not one religion, but all religions; that every historical religion embodies the sacred personality of man, announcing his infinite relations to life, duty, destiny; that everywhere we greet essential meanings of the unity of God with man, of fate, freedom and providence; of inspiration and immortality, of practical duties and humanities. For, however different the externals of worship may be, they but envelope common truths that are the birthright of man; and should we be slow to recognize 'how absolutely universal,' as the great German philosopher Lotze says, 'is the extent of the role which mechanism has to play in the structure of the world, but how entirely subordinate is its significance?' Forms 'varying with the tribes of men' are no doubt a prominent constituent element of all religion; but they are only the external clothing. They are, as Tennyson writes,

> Fair garments, plain or rich, and fitting close
> Or flying looselier, warmed but by the heart
> Within them, moved but by the living limb,
> And cast aside, when old, for newer-Forms!
> The spiritual in Nature's market-place,
> The silent alphabet-of-heaven-in-man
> Made vocal,—banners blazoning a Power
> That is not seen and rules from far away,—
> A silken cord let down from Paradise,
> When fine philosophies would fail, to draw
> The crowd from wallowing in the mire of earth

But behind this diversity, there is an essential unity, and

> The Christian bell, the cry from off the mosque,
> And vaguer voices of Polytheism
> Make but one music, harmonizing "Pray".

II. A strange feature of South-Indian Literary History.

The edition of Manikka Vaçagar's *Tiru Vaçagam*, which that ardent adorer of the sweet-voiced Tamil Saraswati—the late Dr. G. U. Pope of Oxford--gave us some years ago, has naturally imparted a stimulus to the study of the life and writings of the sage; and as a result, various appreciations by Indians and Europeans have appeared in literary magazines. As might be expected, in these appreciations attempts have been made to ascertain the date of Manikka Vacagar; and it is curious to note what a confused wilderness of dates we have, presented to us as representing the probable period when Manikka Vacagar lived. It is a peculiar feature of South Indian literary history, that scholars still feel themselves at liberty to advance any date that fancy may suggest to any writer whatever; and it thus happens that a Tamil poet whom one scholar assigns to the first century after Christ is unhesitatingly assigned by another to the 14th century after Christ! This curious phenomenon, it will be impossible to come across anywhere in the whole field of history except in Southern India. That the picture is by no means overdrawn will be evident when we glance at tho various dates assigned to Manikka Vacagar. It seems to be almost an understood rule or law that the tendency for the Indian scholar is to assign the great names that have enriched his literature to as early a period as well he can; and perhaps the reason for this may be sought in the general belief among us, not unnaturally induced by the glory and glamour of our ancient civilization, that worth and antiquity go hand in hand. The tendency, on the other hand, of the European scholar is just the reverse. It is an article of his creed that the professed antiquity of Tamil literature is only a pious fable; and it is a settled fact with him that Tamil literature grew and flourished only a few centuries ago. For has not Dr. Burnell-and Dr. Burnell ought to know best—issued the *fiat* that the earliest extant work in Tamil literature cannot be older than the 8th century after Christ; and have not eminent scholars like Dr. Rost and Prof. Vinson accepted it without hesitation and even with doci-ity? As a natural result of these conflicting tendencies, the dates arrived at by Indians only serve in the eyes of the European to point the moral that the Indians are deficient in the historic sense ; while the conclusions arrived at by Europeans are regarded by the Indian as only demonstrating their inborn distrust and intolerence of his ancient civilization. Neither has confidence in the results arrived at by the other, though both avowedly pursue 'historical' methods. There should certainly be vital differences in the very fundamentals on which these 'historical' inquiries are based to render such hopelessly irreconcilable results possible. To what extent faulty methods of investigation and the inevitable personal idiosyncracies are severally responsible for the divergent results that stare the student of South Indian literary history in the face, I do not pretend to be able to say ; but to whatever cause the divergence may be due, the position thus created is extremely puzzling.

Turning to Manikka Vacagar, we find that the dates so far assigned to him are as follows :— Mr. S. A. Thirumalai-kolundu Pillai, a Tamil scholar of great ability, who has written a learned thesis on Manikka Vacagar, assigns the sage to the first or second century of the Christian era : and in his conclusion he is followed by the late Pandit V. G. Suryanarayana Sastry B. A.,* and Mr. T. Ponnambalam Pillai, M. R. A. S.‡ Pandit Vedachalam Pillai of the Madras Christian College places him in the 3rd century.§ Elsewhere I have myself endeavoured to make out that Manikka Vacagar should be sought for about the last quarter of the

---

* The Indian Review for April, 1901.

‡ The Malabar Quarterly Review, Vol: III, Page 203.

§ The Christian College Magazine, 1904.

4th century after Christ.† Mr. Wilson holds that the sage 'not improbably' lived in the course of the 7th century.‖ Dr. Pope, the greatest European authority on the *Tiru Vacagam*, believes that there is good reason to suppose that Manikka Vacagar lived somewhere about the 7th or 8th century, and that he cannot have lived later than the 9th century.§ Mr. Innes, late a Judge of the Madras High Court, asserts that Manikka Vacagar lived about the 9th century, because, according to him, our sage was a follower of the school of Sankara Acharya;¶ and Prof: Julien Vinson too will seek for him in the same century * though on different grounds. The Rev. Mr. Goudie states that all that can be said is that the period to which our sage belonged was sometime between the middle of the 8th and the middle of the 10th century.‡ Mr. Nelson affects to be able to tell us the exact year; for he says in his Madura Manual that Manikka Vacagar crossed over to Ceylon in 819 A.C., an assertion based on a statement which he says is found in the *Raja Ratnagiri* that a Caivite priest from the Tamil country crossed over to Ceylon and succeeded in converting the Buddhist King of Ceylon to Caivism 1362 years after the date of Buddha's death.† Mr. Gopinath Rao, M.A. is inclined to place Manikka Vacagar about the beginning of the 11th century or perhaps at the end of the 10th century;‖ and Dr. Reinhold Rost brings him down to the 13th or 14th century after Christ.$ Thus in regard to Manikka Vacagar's date individual opinions have hopelessly drifted without let or hindrance; and it would apparently seem possible to

---

† The Christian College Magazine, September 1901.

‖ Descriptive Catalogue of the Mackenzie collection, Higginbotham's reprint, page 39.

§ Tiru Vacagam: Introduction.

¶ The Indian Magazine & Review. December 1900.
The Imperial & Asiatic Quarterly Review, April 1902.

* The Malabar Quarterly Review Vol: VII, page 112.

‡ The Christian College Magazine, August 1902.

† Madura Manual, I. p. 53.

‖ The Christian College Magazine, June 1905.

$ The Encyclopaedia Britannica, Vol. 25— Tamils.

assign Manikka Vacagar indifferently to the first or to the fourteenth century of the Christian era! This is not a stray instance; for in respect of almost every important date in the ancient history of the Tamil country such vagaries seem possible. When doctors disagree in this manner, we may take it that nobody, however high apparently his authority may be, can afford to be dogmatic on a point of South Indian chronology, in the conditions that now exist; but is it also equally impossible with at least a tolerable approximation to reasonable certainty to arrive at results on such matters that may be generally acceptable? Several of those that have told us when Manikka Vacagar lived have been content with their mere *ipse dixit*; but others have taken considerable trouble to state the reasons that in their view support their conclusions. Not infrequently the premises are bare assumptions, the arguments more ingenious than convincing, and the conclusions no better than bold conjectures; nevertheless such conclusions have their value for purposes of constructive history. Of the various attempts made to ascertain Manikka Vacagar's date, Mr. Gopinatha Rao's is the latest.* Besides being a scholar, Mr. Gopinatha Rao is also an acknowledged Archæologist and Epigraphist, and his conclusions, therefore, are entitled to more than ordinary consideration. In this particular instance, the result arrived at by him is in sharp antagonism to those arrived at or accepted by other Indians, who as we have seen place Manikka Vacagar in the second, third or fourth century after Christ. Though Mr. Gopinatha Rao has not gone quite so far as Dr. Rost in his attempt to make out that Manikka Vacagar was not, as Tamilians fondly suppose, an ancient of the Tamil country, but was really a modern, he has certainly gone much further than every other European that has told us anything about the sage in trying to remove the garb of antiquity in which his countrymen have always delighted to clothe the revered author of the *Tiru Vacagam*. An extravagant prejudice against the antiquity of Tamil literature can alone explain the position of Dr. Rost who would seek for

* Vide the Madras Christian College Magazine, for June, 1905.

Manikka Vacagar in the 13th or 14th century after Christ Both he and Prof. Vinson * have pinned their faith to the fallacious statement of Dr. Burnell in a footnote in his *South Indian Palæography*; and the theory of those scholars of the absolute modernity of extant Tamil literature which according to them arose only after the 8th century after Christ, need not trouble us much as it is admittedly founded on Dr. Burnell's note, which the late Prof. Sundaram Pillai has with his usual lucidity, forcefulness and genial humour conclusively proved to be 'a veritable nest of errors'.† Dr. Rost's statement that Manikka Vacagar belonged to the 13th or 14th century is obviously untenable; for as Mr. Venkayya has shown we find a provision made for reciting Manikka Vacagar's திருச்சாழல் in one of Vikrama Chola's inscriptions; and the date of this Chola's accession is 1118. Besides if Doctor Rost had taken the trouble to look into Tamil sacred literature, he would have found that the *Tiru Vacagam* of Manikka Vacagar had become enshrined in the 8th "*Tiru Murai,*" compiled by Nambi Andar Nambi, a Brahmin priest patronised by Raja Raja Ko Parakesari Varma of the Tanjore inscriptions, whose accession took place in 988 A. C.§ Before Nambi Andar Nambi's days, in other words before the close of the 10th century after Christ, Manikka Vacagar's apotheosis had become complete; and if so, one fails to see by what feat of legerdemain Manikka Vacagar might be made to live in or after the thirteenth or fourteenth century. The case with Mr. Gopinatha Rao, however, stands differently. If he admits that we are to seek for Nambi Andar Nambi at the close of the 10th century, his conclusion that we are to seek for Manikka Vacagar also in the same period may not readily commend itself to the student of Tamil literary history, but it is not unthinkable. I intend therefore to examine in detail the grounds on which Mr. Gopinatha Rao has based his conclusion.

---

* Legends Buddhistes et Djainas.

† Vide "Some Milestones iu the History of Tamil literature," pp. 10-15, edited by the T. A. Society-series No. 3.

§ Ibid. pages 30 et seq., and Mr. V. Venkayya's article in the Christian College Magazine, December, 1904.

These grounds are:—

1. Manikka Vacagar is not mentioned by name by Sundara Murthi Nayanar in his *Tiru Tonda Togai.*

2. There is no allusion to Manikka Vacagar in the three Devaram hymnists.

3. His name does not appear in inscriptions.

4. The Devaram hymnists have not sung lyrics in praise of Perundurai and Uttara Kosa Mangai, (the two shrines consecrated in the *Tiru Vacagam*) which are apparently not old temples. Manikka Vacagar, besides referring to several places in honour of which Devarams have been sung, also makes veiled references to the Devaram hymnists themselves.

5. Manikka Vacagar is conversant with Civa's *Tiru Vilaiyadals,* and these are not referred to by the Devaram hymnists.

6. Manikka Vacagar refers to Chidambaram by the name *Ponnambalam*, which shows that the temple had already been gilded in his days, and he should, therefore, have lived after Parantaka I.

7. Varaguna is referred to by Manikka Vacagar, and this Pandian lived about the first half of the ninth century after Christ.

Of these, grounds 1, 2, 4 & 5 are intended to establish that Manikka Vacagar came after the Devaram hymnists. In postulating this position, Mr. Gopinatha Rao simply brushes aside the accepted tradition—accepted alike by Indian and European scholars—that Manikka Vacagar preceded even the earliest of the Devaram hymnists, Appar or Tiru Navukkarasu. Indeed even Dr. Rost, who as we have seen brings Manikka Vacagar down to the 13th or 14th century, concedes that Appar and Sambandhar came later than Manikka Vacagar.

Dr. Pope in the history of Manikka Vacagar appended to his edition of the *Tiru Vacagam*, feels no hesitation in writing that "it is quite certain that this sage was the first in the long and very remarkable series of devotees of Civan who engaged in the arduous work of recovering the South of India from the Buddhists and Jains;" and he suggests that Manikka Vacagar flourished about 150 to 200 years before Sambandhar. The Tamilian has always accepted as an axiomatic truth that Manikka Vacagar lived long prior to the Devaram hymnists; and this view besides being in consonance with immemorial tradition, and with probabilities, receives considerable confirmation from Tamil literature itself, unless we read it with the set purpose of twisting it to support a preconceived theory. Mr. Gopinatha Rao had perforce to do violence to the established tradition, for otherwise Manikka Vacagar could not have lived after his Varaguna, as he evidently wanted to make out. He had come across an inscription of a Varaguna, and he had tried to place that Pandiyan Prince about the first half of the 9th century. He also found a Varaguna mentioned by Manikka Vacagar; hence Manikka Vacagar must be posterior to the Varaguna of the inscription. Thus had Manikka Vacagar perforce to be placed after the Devaram hymnists, as their dates after considerable agitation have now been practically settled, and it is too late in the day to attack them. Let us now examine if the various reasons advanced by Mr. Gopinatha Rao, to support his view that the Devaram hymnists preceded Manikka Vacagar are so cogent and convincing as to induce us to reject the accepted or orthodox view.

III. Did the Dêvâram Hymnists precede Manikka Vaçagar?

It is first contended that Manikka Vaçagar is not expressly mentioned by name by Sundara in his *Tiru Tonda Togai*; and as Sundara lived in the 9th century, Manikka Vacagar was unknown and therefore probably did not exist before that century. This reasoning has an exact parallel in M. Vinson's *Legendes Buddhistes et D'jainas*, where that learned writer says that Buddha Mitra, the author of *Vira-soliyam*, does not mention *Manimekalai* in his own commentary on that grammer—(Verily, Dr. Burnell has not added his now famous foot-note in vain!)*—and therefore that ancient Tamil epic must have come into existence only after the 12th century, the supposed date of the Buddhist grammarian. Is it, however, certain that Sundara has not referred to Manikka Vacagar in this lyric? The name Manikka Vacagar certainly does not appear; but I venture to maintain that *Poy-adimai-illatha-pulavar*, the opening expression in stanza 7 of the lyric refers to Manikka Vacagar. It cannot be contended that the description will not apply to our sage. It is a well known usage in Tamil to avoid mentioning by name great men round whom an odour of sanctity has settled. Thus in *Manimekalai*, Sattanar refers to Tiru Valluvar not by that name but as *Poy-il-pulavar*. The young sage who at the sight of the Divine Guru beneath the spreading Kurumtham tree at Peruntural renounced the plentitude of wordly pomp, power and position and felt himself one in soul with the Infinite Eternal, may not unnaturally be reverently referred as Poy-adimai-illatha-pulavar by a Civa devotee that came several centuries afterwards. I am not aware that there is any particular

* Elements of South Indian Palaeography, p. 127.

reason to regard the expression used by Sundara Murti as necessarily embracing a 'rather elastic class of devotees' as Mr. Gopinatha Rao believes. I hold it denotes no class at all, as the expressions in the 10th verse of the same lyric do; it is simply intended to denote a single individual whom Sundara Murti Nayanar's contemporaries could easily have identified. The position occupied by the verse which begins with the expression we are considering, also favours the view that the plural suffix is merely honorific and that Sundara meant it to apply to a specific individual. If that be conceded, and it seems to me most Tamilians will be prepared to concede it, then the only question is: whom did the Nayanar mean by it? It should denote a great sage who was also a great poet, a *Jivan-mukta* who in his life and his writings testified to the Supreme value and the saving grace of Divine Service; and who better satisfies this description than Manikka Vacagar? I would just add that Manikka Vacagar's conception of the nature and function of Civan was heterodox from the standpoint of Sundara Murti Nayanar or indeed of the other Devaram hymnists. God's manifestation as a groom or a hunter or a fisherman, much less as a cow or a dove or a hog was unthinkable to the hymnists of the Devaram collection; and Sundarar perhaps felt that Manikka Vacagar whose theology made it possible for him to assert that his Divine Master made himself manifest even in those forms to perform various acts of grace, was outside the pale of orthodox Caivism and therefore he dared not mention him by name in this lyric composed in honour of orthodox Caiva devotees, but contented himself with making a reference to the sage by employing the descriptive term *Poy-adimai-illâtha-pulavar*. To my mind, therefore, there is no doubt that Sundara Murti refers to Manikka Vacagar expressly by the term *Poy-adimai-illâtha-pulavar*. In making this statement I have not forgotten that my interpretation is opposed to Nambi Andar Nambi's interpretation of the term in his *Tiru-tonda Tiru-anthathi*. In stanza 49 of that poem, Nambi Andar Nambi explains *Poy-adimai-illatha-pulavar* as comprising the forty-nine poets including Kapilar, Baranar and Nakkirar, who belonged to the third Sangam or

Academy, and many other poets who have sung in sweet verse the praises of the God of Madura. According to Nambi Andar Nambi, therefore, *Poy-adimai-illatha-pulavar* denotes a class of devotees and not a single devotee. I venture, however, though with great hesitation and diffidence, to believe that Nambi's interpretation of the term is incorrect. In the first place all the forty-nine poets of the third Academy were certainly not Caiva devotees. Kapilar, Baranar and Nakkirar, some of whose writings are incorporated in the eleventh *Tiru-Murai* may be included among devotees; but their brother-bards of the Academy, though they may be entitled to a high place among poets, can possess no claim to be regarded as devotees of Civan. Indeed many of them were Jains or Buddhists; and apparently Nambi should be held to have forgotton this fact when he claimed all the forty-nine poets as devotees of Civan. Besides, one might well ask what necessity there was to refer to the poets of the Madura Academy and others by a generic term right in the middle of a string of individual names of devotees, while in the tenth verse of the *Tiru-tonda-togai*, which consists entirely of generic terms, Sundara uses expressions elastic enough to embrace all poets that may possess any claim to be considered Caiva devotees. Sundara could certainly not have been so hard pressed to find names to fill in his list as to be driven to the inartistic device of employing more than one term to denote practically the same class. Yet again, we find Nambi Andar Nambi himself telling us in stanza 87 of his *Anthathi* that Sundara Murti in his *Tiru-tonda-togai* has enumerated in eleven verses seventy-two great devotees consisting of *Sixty-three individual names* and nine classes. Now if we count the names of the devotees individually mentioned in the *Tiru-tonda-togai* we will find that there are only *Sixty-two* excluding *Poy-adimai-illatha-pularar;* and it is only by regarding *Poy-adimai-illatha-pulavar* also as denoting a specific individual that we can make up the 63 devotees, who, as Nambi admits, are specifically mentioned by Sundarar. No doubt we will then have only *eight and not nine* classes; and this mistake can be easily explained. Sundara Murti Nayana had sung of 63 individual saints, thus giving currency to the expression "*The Sixty-three*" (அறுபத்து மூவர்) and had also in his hymn employed a whole verse of general expressions to include all that might have been left out. Nambi Andar Nambi retained the traditional 'Sixty-three', for by his time it must have become traditional; and little remembering that the figure 63 would be obtained only by regarding *Poy-adimai-illatha-pulavar* as denoting an individual devotee, he inadvertently mistook the term to denote a class, and with the ingenuity of the commentator so twisted the expression as to enable him to give a plausible, though by no means a satisfactory explanation. For, after all, Nambi Andar Nambi in his *Tiru-tonda-tiru-anthathi* is only in the position of a commentator on Sundara Murti's *Tiru-tonda-togai*; and it is not improbable that though Sundara ment to denote by the term *Poy-adimai-illatha-pulavar* a particular individual, Nambi mistook him and understood him wrongly. Such instances are not rare. The great commentator Nachchinarkkiniyar unable to understand a passage in one of the *Patthu Pattu* describing agricultural operations in Kuttanad with which he was not familiar, has with great ingenuity so twisted the passage and dislocated the expressions as to render it possible for him to attach a meaning to it consistent with his own experience of agriculture on the east coast. I repeat, therefore, that to my mind there is no doubt that by *Poy-adimai-illatha-Pulavar* Sundara refers to Manikka Vacagar. I am strengthened in this conclusion when I note that our sage is referred to in the earlier Tiru Vilayadal Puranam by such terms as மெய்யடியான் and பாடன்மா முனிவர்.

I may, however, add that whether we hold Sundara makes an explicit or even implied reference to Manikka Vacagar or not, Appar, the earliest of the Devaram hymnists makes specific reference to our sage in his lyrics, as I shall show presently. This leads us to the consideration of the next allegation that there is no allusion to Manikka Vacagar in the works of the three hymnists, an assertion that will be received with unmitigated surprise by Tamilians. Tamil scholars have till now maintained that in one of Tiru Nâvukkarasar's hymns where he mentions the well-known Divine

Sport of the transformation of foxes into horses, that sage was making a reference to a reputed incident in Manikka Vacagar's life. The verse occurs in one of Appar's lyrics sung at Tiru Arur, and runs as follows :—

நரியைக் குதிரை செய்வானு நரகரைத்தேவு செய்வானும்
விரதங்கொண்டாட வல்லானும் விச்சின்றி நாறு செய்வானு
முரசதிர்ந் தானை முன்னோட முன்பணிந் தன்பர் சளேத்த
அரவரைச் சாத்தி நின்றானு மாரூ ரமர்ந்த வம்மானே.

Everybody knows the story of Manikka Vacagar's conversion, the great story of his sudden passage from darkness into light. He had been sent by his sovereign master to purchase a stud of horses for Royal use, and it was in that trip that he met at Perunturai his mystic Guru, who initiated him and wrought in him that great transformation which made him Civan's very own. The young sage having forgotten the mission on which he had been sent by the king, and spent the treasure intended for the purchase of his horses on his Guru and his disciples, the king caused him to be seized and thrown into prison * whence he sent pathetic prayers to the great god that had manifested himself to him at Perunturai. Tradition says that the lament then uttered by the sage is preserved in செத்திலாப்பத்து and பிரார்த்தனைப்பத்து and the ruling ideas of those decades are worthy of note in this connection. In the former the young sage unable to endure his anguish and suffering, cries out

இறக்கி லேன்உனைப் பிரிந்தினி யிருக்க
　என்செய் கேன்இது செய்கவென் றருளாய்
சிறைக்க ணேபுன லிலவிய வயல்சூழ்
　திருப்பெ ருந்துறை மேவிய சிவனே.

---

* வேதனைப்பட விருத்திய வெங்கொடுஞ் சிறையாற்
போதநீடிய கடுந்துயர் பொறுக்கமாட்டாமல்
ஆதிநாதனை நினைந்தழு தலர்ச்சணீர் சொரிய
வாதவூரரும் புலம்புவார் வாசக மோதி.

Vêmbattûrar—Tiru Vilaiyadal. 28 (6)

He feels that the great Lord of Perunturai is with-holding his saving Grace from him and he pathetically asks:

> என்னைக்
> கோதுமாட்டி நின்குரைகழல் காட்டிக்
> குறிக்கொள்கென்று நின்றொண்டரிற் கூட்டாய்
> யாது செய்வதென்றிருந்தனன் மருந்தே
> அடியனே னிடர்ப்படுவது மினிதே?

In his humiliation and misery, where else can he seek refuge except in his Divine master's boundless grace? He cries in supplication:

> Thy loving ones the sea of bliss attain. Is it then meet
> That I, low dog, with added pains and pining sore should bide?
> Master, do Thou thyself give grace, I pray, I faint, I fail!
> Hasten O Light that darkness,' fore thy mercy's beam may flee!

Tiruvacagam XXXII, Stanza 7.

Is it meet that Civan's slave should languish like an alien (அடியேனு மயலார்போல அயர்வேனோ) and weep aloud as one forsaken by god (சேடனுகி நின்றுறவழைப்பேனோ); and if he appeal will the merciful Father with-hold His Grace and allow His servant to droop, all forlorn, like a withered tree? (வாடி வாடி வழியற்றேன் வற்றன்மரம்போனிற்பேனோ) and so the sage sends forth a touching prayer from his prison,

> கலந்து நின்னடி யாரோ டன்று வாளா களித்திருந்தேன்
> புலர்ந்து போன காலங்கள் புகுந்து நின்று நிடர்ப்பின்னாள்
> உலர்ந்து போனே னுடையானே உலவா இன்பச்சுடர்காண்பா
> னலந்து போனே னருள்செய்யா யார்வங் கூர வடியேற்கே.

Tiruvacagam XXXII, Stanza 1.

and in response Civan is said to have performed a miracle which saved Manikka Vacagar and established his sanctity as a Caiva saint for ever. Moved by the appeals of Manikka Vacagar, He transformed jackals into horses and delivered them to the Pandyan king. This miracle or sport of Civa has always been associated in the Tamilian's mind with the life-story of our sage. The two *Tiru-Vilayadal-Puranams,* whatever their historical value may be, may at least be taken as faithfully embodying the tradition of ages as preserved in and believed by the Tamil country. In the investigation of the past we have to turn largely to traditions, both oral and written, as forming a legitimate source of empirical material for constructive history. When for centuries a tradition has been unhesitatingly and consistently associated with a particular person, some ground more convincing than a mere freak of fancy is necessary to justify our attempt to dissociate that tradition from that person. It has long been the traditional belief of the Tamil people that this particular sport of Civa was manifested for Manikka Vacagar's benefit, and the tradition well fits in with the general story of the sage's life. It is only natural to suppose, unless there is something repugnant in the context, that when the tradition is mentioned a reference to the person with whom the tradition has been uniformly associated is intended. Ordinarily, therefore, when Appar in one of his lyrics sung at Tiru-Arur mentions the Divine act of the transformation of jackals into horses, he would be held to refer to a well-understood incident in Manikka Vacagar's life. This is the view entertained by Tamilians as a class; but Mr. Gopinatha Row feels it will be inconvenient to accept it, and so rejects it on the following grounds:

i. that the allusions made in the Tiru-Vacagam to this incident do not bear out the tradition; and

ii. that if the reference in Appar's verse is to the miracle performed for the benefit of Manikka Vacagar, we should also be able to say, to what incidents in the life of Manikka Vacagar or of any other saint the references in the latter part of the verse relate.

Now it is well-known that Manikka Vacagar refers to this miracle as an actual fact accomplished by Civan; and he refers to it more than once in his *Tiru-Vacagam*. It would have been very much better if instead of making a bold statement as Mr. Gopinatha Row has done that the sage's allusions to the incident 'distinctly contradict' the accounts given in the *Tiru-Vilaiyadal-Puranam* and the *Vatharurar-Puranam*, he had actually told us what the contradictions were that influenced him in his rejection of the tradition as false. If he means to suggest that the references found in the *Tiru-Vacagam* do not show that the miracle was really an incident in Manikka Vacagar's life, I conceive that there may be two opinions about it. In his *Kirli-Tiru-Agaval* or the sacred song of Civan's renowned Acts, Manikka Vacagar writes

அரியொடு பிரமற் களவறி யொண்ணான்
நரியைக் குதிரை யாக்கிய நன்மையும்
ஆண்டு கொண்டருள அழகுறு திருவடி
பாண்டி யன்றனக் குப்பரி மாவிற்
றீண்டு கனகம் இசையப் பெறாஅ
தாண்டா னெங்கோ னருள்வழி யிருப்பத்
தூண்டு சோதி தோன்றிய தொன்மையும்
அந்தண னாகி யாண்டு கொண்டருளி
இந்திர ஞாலங் காட்டிய வியல்பும்
மதுரைப் பெருநன் மாநக ரிருந்து
குதிரைச் சேவக னாகிய கொள்கையும்

and in திருப்பொன்னூசல் occurs the line

ஞால மிசைப்பரிமேற்கொண்டு நமையாண்டான்.

We are yet to be convinced that these lines do not suggest that Manikka Vacagar at least sincerely believed that the great Civan who, in the form of a Brahmin Guru, had made Him His own, had for his benefit wrought the magic illusion of transforming jackals into horses and, proceeding with them to Madura in the guise of a horse's groom, left them with the Pandyian King. Elsewhere too, in *Anantha-Malai*, Stanza 7, Manikka Vacagar writes:

நரியைக் குதிரைப் பரியாக்கி ஞால மெல்லா நிகழ்வித்து
பெரிய தென்னன் மதுரையெல்லாம் பிச்சதேற்றும் பெருந்துறையாய்.

The sage in these lines distinctly states that Civan by His wondrous magic in transforming jackals into chargers *has filled* the great city of Madura with ecstasy; and the language clearly shows that Manikka Vacagar regarded the miracle as a contemporaneous event that occurred in Madura as a manifestation of Civa's grace. Again in *Tiru-Ammanai* he says:

பந்தம் பறியப் பரிமேற் கொண்டான் றந்த
அந்தமிலா வானந்தம் பாடுதுங்காண் அம்மானாய்!

and the first line, as anybody can see, is a felicitous *double entendre*; பந்தம signifying both confinement in prison and the bonds of existence Yet again in திருவேசறவு the sage sings in language that leaves little doubt about the object of, and the occasion for, this divine sport:

இரும்புதரு மனத்தேனை யீர்த்தீர்த்தென் என்புருக்கிக்
கரும்புதரு சுவையெனக்குக் காட்டினையுன் கழலிணைக
ளொருங்குதிரை யுலவுசடை யுடையானே! நரிகளெல்லாம்
பெருங்குதிரை யாக்கியவா றன்றேயுன் பேரருளே.

So too in திருவார்த்தை:

அடியோங்களுய்ய
ஆடலமர்ந்த பரிமாவேறி ஐயன்பெருந்துறை யாதி யந்நா
ளேடர்களை எங்குமாண்டு கொண்ட வியல்பறிவாரெம்பிரா னாவா
ரே.

The frequency with which and the manner in which the sage refers to this miracle or sport of Civa in his *Tiru Vacagam* lends considerable support to the traditional belief that it was manifested by the Deity for Manikka Vacagar's special benefit. Vembaturar's *Tiru Vilayadal Puranam* is at least more than nine centuries old; and in it this Divine Sport is described as having been performed by Civan to release Manikka Vacagar from prison. That was the traditional belief even when Venbatur Nambi wrote his work. The words in which he describes the Deity's manifestation of grace in transforming jackals into horses are almost identical with the expressions used by Appar in the verse already quoted from his Tiru Arur lyric. Vembatur Nambi writes :—

மன்னிய வுலகு தன்னில் வித்தின்றி நாறு செய்வோன்
நன்னெறி யில்லாப் பொல்லா நரகரை தேவுத்செய்வோன்
மன்னிய நரிக டம்மை மறுசெலாம் வாவி யேறித்
தென்னன்முன் குதிரையாக செய்புதோன்றுமல் விட்டான்.

There cannot be the least doubt that the author of the *Tiru Vilayadal* when he wrote the above stanza had Appar's verse in mind; and he took Appar to refer in the opening lines of his verse to this particular *Tiru Vilayadal* performed for the special benefit of Manikka Vacagar. The foremost Tamil scholar of the present day Pandit V. Swaminatha Iyer also is of opinion that Appar's words நரியைக் குதிரை செய்வான் contain an allusion to this particular *Tiru Vilayadal.* In these circumstances one does not easily see why the tradition should be discredited,. and the legitimate inference drawn from Appar's reference to the miracle denied or questioned. It is, however, suggested as a difficulty that if we take the opening words in Appar's verse to refer to an alleged miracle in Manikka Vacagar's life, the words that succeed should also be taken as referring to specific incidents in the life of some saint or other; a conclusion which is not inevitable or even necessary; but even if that be a necessary conclusion, it seems to me that there is no real difficulty. The verse describes Civan as also

(1) நரகரைத் தேவு செய்வான்.
(2) விரதங் கொண்டாட வல்லான்.
and (3) விச்சின்றி நாறு செய்வான்;

and these expressions, one can easily see, contain references to well-known *lilas* or sports of Civan. The first of these expressions நரகரைத் தேவு செய்வான் refers to the story recited in the twenty-sixth *Tiru Vilayadal* by Paranjoti Munivar - a story found also in the older *Tiru Vilayadal Puranam.* The hero of that story had been guilty of an unthinkable sin, the heinous nature of which may be gauged from the followiug language used about him by Sivan's consort:

"இக்கொடியோன் செய்த பாவத்துக் களவில் காலம் வெய்ய நா லேழுகோடி நரகிடை வீழ்ந்தானேனு முய்வகை யிலாத பாவி."

(*Tiru Vilayadal* XXVI, Stanza 34.)

and நின்னுமஞ் சொன்னோர் வருக்கமு நரகில் வீழக் கருதி நீ செய்த பாவம்.

(*Tiru Vilayadal* XXVI, Stanza 31.)

—langauge which makes one shudder! This monster of iniquity, the enormity of whose sin was such that not only he but even those that uttered his vile name and their family deserved to be consigned to eternal hell-fire, was by the all-embracing grace of Civan saved from hell, and he ultimately became in consequence one of the children of light that have their abode close to the feet of the Lord. In describing the transformation, Paranjoti Munivar writes:

பாதகங் கழிந்து தெய்வப் பார்ப்பன வடிவமானான்.

Tiru Vilayadal XXVI, Stanza 38.

and தற்பர வறிவா னந்தத் தனியுரு வுடைய சோதி
பொற்பத மருங்கிற் புக்கான் புண்ணிய மறையோ னம்மா.

Tiru Vilayadal XXVI, Stanza 39.

So far about the *lila* alluded to in the first expression. Turning to the next expression விரதங்கொண்டாட வல்லான், the allusion is patent. It obviously refers to Pinjnakan Kûttu (பிஞ்ஞகன் கூத்து), the *Natanam* or dance that Civan set up in opposition to Kali. Perhaps there may also be in it allusions to the stories narrated as the sixth and the twenty-fourth *Tiru Vilayadal* in Paranjoti Munivar's work. There remains, then, only the last of the three descriptive phrases, விச்சின்றி நாறு செய்வான்; and in this expression there is a reference to an act of grace manifested by Civan on behalf of Tiru Nâlai-pôvâr, the well known Pariah saint. The story is well-known to almost every child in the Tamil country that on one occasion Tiru Nâlai-pôvâr or Nanthan, in his devotional frenzy, so completely forgot himself and the work alloted to him by his Brahmin master, that he allowed the field that he was to have tilled to lie fallow, while the fields under the care of other servants were under cultivation. The harvest was approaching; but Nanthan was apparently unconscious of it and of the neglected condition of his field. The *Arudra* festival at Chidambaram was also approaching; and he was yearning to go to Thillai for the sacred festival. One evening before the harvest Nanthan appeared before his master to obtain permission to proceed to Chidambaram; but the latter told him sharply that he had nothing to do with Chidambaram, and that unless at the harvest the field entrusted to him for cultivation yielded as good a crop as the rest, things would go very hard with him. The poor slave however extracted a promise from his master that he would be allowed to proceed to the holy city for *Arudra* if he succeeded in showing good crops on his field before that date. The pariah devotee went home, and throughout the night he poured out his very soul in prayer to the Great Dancer in Thillai 's Golden Hall, beseeching His grace and His help to render it possible for him to proceed to Thillai for the festival; and the next morning when Nanthan went to his field, he found to his inexpressible joy that his prayer had been answered by Civan. For lo! a miracle had been wrought overnight. Unseen hands had during the night raised a bumper crop on his field; and the waving corn stood ready to be harvested. Nanthan hurried to his master to communicate the welcome news; and not only did he get the requisite permission to go to the holy shrine that he had so much longed for, but he also secured in his master a disciple and a devotee of his beloved Nataraja. Thus we find that all the descriptive epithets applied to Civan by Appar in the verse we have been considering are satisfactorily explicable as referring to well-known *lilas* or manifestations of divine grace. The fancied difficulty therefore in taking the opening words in Appar's verse to refer to a specific sport of Sivan manifested for Manikka Vacagar's benefit absolutely vanishes. This, however, is not the only reference to our sage in Appar; but it is best to examine the cogency of the remaining grounds advanced to establish Manikka Vacagar's alleged appearance after the Devaram hymnists, before I refer to the other passages in Appar which contain allusions to our sage.

We are next told that neither Perunturai nor Uttara Kosa Mangai has formed the subject of a single hymn from Jnana Sambandhar, Appar or Sundarar; and they would not have omitted these shrines if they had really been sung about before their days by Manikka Vacagar. Hence we are asked to hold that Manikka Vacagar added these two shrines to the list of sacred places subsequent to the days of the three Nâyanârs. In the first place, is it contended that the 791 or 796 lyrics that we now possess represent the entire body of lyrics actually sung by the hymnists? There is conclusive authority for holding that the actual number of hymns sung by the three Nayanars was 10,300, of which only 796 have now survived;* and where is the warrant then for holding that they had not sung about Tiru Perunturai or Uttara Kosa Mangai? Besides, if we look into the Devaram, we will notice that Sundarar the latest of the Nayanars has not devoted one single hymn to Tiru-Alavai or Madura while Appar has two and Sambandhar has nine hymns about that holy shrine. Similarly among the Devaram hymns relating to Rameswaram we find one is by Appar and the remaining two by Sambandhar, while Sundarar has not sung about it at all. So again while Tiru Naraiyur, Tiru Palanam, Tiru Mayiladuthurai, Tiru Annamalai, Tiru Gokaranam and various other places have been the subjects of hymns by both Appar and Sambandhar, not one of them has had the honour of eliciting even a single lyric in its praise from Sundarar. Following the line of reasoning adopted by Mr. Gopinatha Row we might hold that Madura, Rameswaram and the other places we have mentioned could not have sprung into importance as Caiva shrines before Sundarar's days, as otherwise he would have sung about them; and they should have been only subsequently added by Appar and Sambandhar to the long list of consecrated places he had already celebrated in his lyrics, and those two saints therefore could have come only after him. I shall not multiply such analogies as even one is quite enough to show the real worth of such an argument. Nor is Mr. Gopinatha Row's statement that neither Perunturai nor Uttara Kosa Mangai is sung about in the Devaram grounded on fact. From the Devaram we find that Perunturai and Uttara Kosa Mangai were both Caiva shrines of repute even in the days of Appar.

---

* *Kuppusami Mudaliar's article in* 1st *Sen-Tamil* p.p. 439—447.

In the Sixth Tirumurai, Appar specially mentions Peruntura,i both in his *Kshetrak-kovai* and his *Tiruadaivu*, as one of the principal shrines where the Lord of Kailas dwells. No doubt he does not devote an entire lyric to its praise; but that is because he had not visited the shrine. All the same it was to him a consecrated shrine like Chidambaram, Shiyali, Tiru Arur or any other holy place he had sung about; and is it unreasonable to suppose that the sanctity that had already gathered round the name of Perunturai in Appar's days was at least in part due to its association with Manikka Vasagar's spiritual conversion? As for Uttara Kosa Mangai the name apparently does not appear in the Devaram hymns. Neverthless it is certain it was not unknown to Appar as a holy shrine; for in one of his lyrics there occurs the expression அதியரைய மங்கையமர்ந்தான் which contains an obvious allusion to a well-known *Tiru Vilayadal* associated with Uttara Kosa Mangai. There can thus be no doubt that the sanctity of both Perunturai and Uttara Kosa Mangai dates from a period earlier than even the days of Appar. There is also another circumstance that helps us to hold that Tiru Perunturai was already in the days of the earlier Devaram hymnists a place of known and established sanctity. One of Tiru Jnana Sambandhar's lyrics is in honour of திருப்பேணு பெருந்துறை and obviously the verbal adjective பேணு was added to the name of the town to differentiate it from a well known Tiru Perunturai. Indeed I am not sure that the name பேணு பெருந்துறை was not itself suggested by the occurence of this identical expression in the *Tiruvacagam*, where in *Tiru Ammanai* we read in line 58, பெண்ணொருபாகனைப் பேணு பெருந்துறையில் and in line 110 பிஞ்ஞகனைப் பேணு பெருந்துறையில் மன்னனை, and in this doubt I am strengthened by the fact that in the only two lines in which Sambandhar employs the expression பேணு பெருந்துறை in his lyric he seems to be only reproducing the same association of ideas as we find in the two lines from Manikka Vacagar above noticed. If Tiru Perunthurai has, as I shall attempt to show presently, to be sought for in the present Malayalam country, that will account for the absence of specific hymns in its honour by Appar or Sambhandhar who did not visit that country at all, or by Sundarar who visited only Tiru-Anchai-Kalam.

In his desire to make his position secure, Mr. Gopinatha Row does not hesitate to lean on another broken reed. He intends to suggest, for he does not expressly say so, that there are more shrines consecrated in Manikka Vacagar's poetry than in the Devaram hymns; and from this supposititious circumstance he concludes 'that Manikka Vacagar came only after the Nayanars.' As a matter of fact the number of places that have hymns assigned to them in the Devaram is 274; and there are in the Devaram hymns 249 other places casually mentioned, thus making up a total of 523. There are only two shrines really or if we include also Tillai and Tiru Kalum Kunram in honour of which seperate lyrics are sung, four that are consecrated in the *Tiru Vacagam*, and about a dozen or two casually mentioned in that work; and some of these are also found in the Devaram. It is conceded that with the growth of devotional activity, each succeeding generation would see a larger number of shrines spring into fame. The legitimate inference therefore is that Manikka Vacagar, who has sung of an inconsiderably small number of places, long preceded the Devaram hymnists in whose works the temples that are sung about increase considerably in number. A disinterested scholar like Dr. Pope, who has devoted many long years to the study of Tamil religious literature, could write: "The shrines he visited (Manikka Vacagar) were however very few in comparison of those said to have been hallowed by the presence of Sambandhar and the other saints of the following cycle." This is an obvious conclusion that will be readily accepted by Tamilians and yet Mr. Gopinatha Row has strangely shut his eyes to this patent fact.

Mr. Gopinatha Row has other surprises for us in this part of his argument. Consistency, as everybody knows is the quality of small minds; and Mr. Gopinatha Row is not consistent. He will not accept the explanation for it 'would hardly satisfy anyone' that Manikka Vacagar is included in a generic expression occuring in Sundarar's *Tiru Thonda Togai*; nor will he allow us to infer that by a particular expression, Appar makes a reference to a well-understood incident in the personal history of Manikka Vacagar, unless we can also explain to what incidents the remaining expressions in the verse referred. When. it, however, suits his purpose he can write that in that Atlantic of an expression *Tondar* (தொண்டர்) "one can easily see Manikka Vacagar allude to the Devaram hymners!" I confess I do not even with difficulty see it at all; and I am afraid many others will be in the same sad predicament with me.

With a *naivete* almost inimitable he states that the fact that our sage mentions the names of Kannappar and Chandeswarar bears out his conclusion. Unless it is intended to suggest that Kannappar and Chandeswarar also came after the Devaram hymnists there can be no point or relevancy in this statement. As a matter of fact both these Caiva saints were long anterior to even Appar whose lyrics refer specifically to the events of their life, and the miracles performed by Civan for their salvation. That being so, by what process of logic can it be made out that because Manikka Vacagar mentions Kannappar and Chandeswarar he should have come only after the Devaram writers? Kannappar and Chandeswarar and Karaikal Ammai are three of the very oldest names among Caiva Saints, and their legends are apparently connected even with pre-aryan usages; and the fact that Manikka Vacagar mentions only these devotees, is almost proof positive that he lived long prior to the other saints, the Devaram authors included. " The great revival and spread of Caivism is due to certain saints or devotees who were men of great devotion, unwearied activity, and remarkable power. The first of these was Manikka Vacagar,............................probably about a century later arose Jnana Sambandhar and the various lesser devotees whose legends are collected, and amplified and idealized in the *Peria Puranam*." This is the view of Dr. Pope, and it is shared as we have seen by even Dr. Rost. Indeed that is the generally accepted view; and almost every body is satisfied that it is correct except Mr. Gopinatha Row. While others have held that Manikka Vacagar's influence is perceptible in Appar's fervent hymns, Mr. Gopinatha Row reverses the position by saying that there are passages in the *Tiru-Vacagam* that are close imitations of the Devaram hymns; and he cites in support one of those very passages that are relied on by those holding the orthodox view. He professes to see in such apparently harmless lines as

"கழுமலவ தனிற் காட்சி கொடுத்தும்"

and "தேனமர்சோலைத் திருவாரூரின்
ஞானந்தன்னை நல்கிய நன்மையும்."

allusions to the story of Sambandhar and Sundarar respectively. Of course to base an argument on Appar's "நரியைக் குதிரை செய்வான்" in favour of Manikka Vacagar's priority to the Devaram hymnists is 'very unsatisfactory !' but to ask you to believe that in the first of the lines above quoted Manikka Vacagar refers to Sambandhar and in the other extract to Sundramurti—well, that is a different story altogether !. After all, by what necessity should we see these references in these lines? Following his reasoning elsewhere we may ask: For whose sake were wrought the other acts of Civa's manifestations mentioned in the succeeding lines? Besides tradition says that the divine figure first manifested to Sambandhar was that of Civan's consort and not Civan; and the place where the manifestation occured has a consecrated name in Tamil literature. It is Tiru Piramapuram, and not Kalumalam. No doubt Pirampuram and Kalumalam are different names for Shiyali,—and I am aware that Sambandhar refers to himself as கழுமல முதுபதி கவுணியன், "the Koundinya Brahmin of the ancient town of Kalumalam." But in the Devaram there are sung by Sambandhar himself separate sets of hymns for Piramapuram and Kalumalam; and if Manikka Vasagar intended to refer to an incident associated in sacred literature with the name of Piramapuram, it is only reasonable to suppose that he would not in that connection mention the name Kalumalam.

With regard to the alleged reference to Sundaramurti, it is even more fanciful. Sundaramurti is no doubt called *Tiru Arur-Nambi.* What is the warrant for saying that 'the conferring of wisdom on Sundaramurti,' was at Tiru Arur? Sundarar himself tells us in *Tiru Navalar Pathigam* that Civan blessed him with spiritual wisdom and made him His own at Tiru Vennai Nallur. In eight of the eleven verses comprising that hymn, he repeats வெண்ணெய்நல்லூரில் வைத்தென்னை யாளுங் கொண்டார்.

He is the only one among the Devaram hymnists that has sung in praise of Tiru Vennai Nallur. No doubt Tiru Arur had special associations for Sundarar; but the spiritual significance of the place seems to have appealed more to Appar and Sambandhar who have in all devoted twenty-six hymns to that shrine than to Sundarar who has sung only eight hymns in its praise. In one of his hymns Sundarar sings

> நறுமலர் பூவு நீரும் நாடொறும் வணங்குவோர்க்கு
> அறிவினைக் கொடுக்கு மாரூ ரப்பனே!

but this certainly has no special significance in respect of himself. It is thus clear that except in imagination there is no allusion in the Tiru Vacagam to the authors of the Devaram; and Mr. Gopinatha Row's statement to the contrary is only an instance of 'the wish being father to the thought.'

It is next alleged that Manikka Vacagar is conversant with a number of *Tiru Vilayadals* relating to Madura, while the Nayanmars are unacquainted with them. These Divine sports are collected in the *Tiru Vilayadal Puranam* and it is argued that our sage should be placed some time before or after the writing of that work! This is no doubt an argument; but I am not sure if it was intended to be treated seriously. Among the various sports of Civan collected even in the earlier of the two *Tiru Vilayadal Puranams* are found those that are expressly stated to have been performed for the special benefit of Manikka Vacagar himself. Every body knows that it is the floating traditions of long ago that are collected in such works, and some of the legends there preserved must have

5

gained currency in the Tamil country from their occurence in Manikka Vacagar's works. It will therefore be more consonant with reason and probabilities to hold that Manikka Vacagar preceded by several centuries even the earlier Tiru Vilayadal Puranam to justify the mention in that work of miracles alleged to have been performed and obviously believed by several preceding generations to have been performed by Civan for the sake of our saint. It is, however, alleged that the Madura *Tiru Vilayaduls* were unknown to the Devaram hymnists. The sports of Civan mentioned in Manikka Vacagar's works are, as might be expected, associated with Madura; and it is only natural and reasonable to expect a larger reference to such *Tiru Vilayaduls* in the works of our sage than in the lyrics of the Devaram hymnists who belonged to the Chola country. It is not a fact, however, that in the Devaram hymns there is no allusion to the *Tiru Vilayaduls* performed in Madura; for they are freely referred to. The very name "Tiru Alavai" by which both Appar and Sambandhar refer to Madura contains a reference to a well-known *Tiru Vilayadal* described by both Perumparra Puliyur Nambi and Paranjoti Munivar. In Tiru Jnana Sambandhar's lyrics we come across the following lines:—

> "ஆடலேற்றினான் கூடலாலவாய்"
> "கொட்டிசைந்த வாடலாய் கூடலால வாயிலாய்"
> "பாணனிசை பத்திமையாற் பாடுதலும் பரிந்தளித்தான்"
> "பட்டிமன் றென்னன்"
> "தாரமுய்த்தது பாணற்கருளொடே"
> "ஆலவாயரன் கையது வீணையே"
> "புன்சடை பின்றயங்க வாடுவாய்"
> "நால்வேதமும் பொருள்களுமருளி யங்கயற் கண்ணிதன்னோடு
> மமர்ந்த வாலவாயாவது மிதுவே"
> "உம்பருநாக ருலகந் தானு மொலிகடல் சூழ்ந்த வுலகத் தோரு
> மம்புத நாட்களானீடுங்கூட லால்வாயின்க ணமர்ந்த வாறே."
> "அதிரவீசி யாடுவா யழகனே"

These are only illustrative extracts but they will suffice to show that Sambandhar was not unacquainted with several of the *Tiru Vilayaduls* relating to Madura. Shall we therefore say that Sambandhar lived after the authors of the *Tiru-Vilayadal Puranams*? Turning to Appar's lyrics we find the following lines:—

"மணியார் வைகைத் திருக்கோட்டி னின்றதோர் திறமுந் தோன்றும்'
"நன்பாட்டுப்புலவனாய்ச் சங்கமேறி, நற்கனகக் கிழிதருமிக் கருளி
னோன்காண்"
"வளைவிலியா யெல்லோர்க்கு மருள்செய்தானை"
"அதியரைய மங்கை யமர்ந்தான் றன்னை"
"பால விருத்தரு மானார் தாமே"
"பாலவிருத்தனுமானான் கண்டாய்"
"விருத்தனாய் பாலனாகி", "பாலனாய் விருத்தனாகி"
"நிலமருவி நீரோடக் கண்டான்றன்னை"
"தேவனைத் தென்கூடற் றிருவாலவாய்ச்
சிவனடியே சிந்திக்கப் பெற்றே னானே"
"குழகனே கோலவில்லி கூத்தனே"
"வேதனைம் மிகுவீணையில் மேவியகீதனை"

These extracts should suffice to show that the earliest of the Devaram hymnists was very familiar with the *Tiru Vilayadals* performed in Madura. Indeed, references to these *Tiru Vilayadals* are found in works written long before the days of the Devaram hymns; for example we find allusions to them in the *Chilap-adhigaram*, a work that belongs to the close of the first or the beginning of the second century of the Christian era. Did Ilam-Ko Adigal also obtain his knowledge of the *Tiru Vilayadals* from Vembathur Nambi or Paranjothi Munivar? Every student of Appar's Devaram hymns knows how frequently that saint refers to Civan's acts of grace in giving salvation to a spider at Kalahasti. That legend is found mentioned in the *Skanda Puranam* by Kachiappar. Kachiappar read his *Skanda Puranam* before the assembly of Pandits in the last quarter of the eighth century; and Appar according to this lyric cannot be earlier than the ninth century! This is a highly consecrated legend; and it is maintained that it is one of the three miracles after which Kalahasti has been named. If this story is not referred to by Sambandhar or Sundarar, shall we say it was unknown to them, and Appar who freely alludes to it came only after them?

IV. The incorrectness of the identification of Tiru-perum-turai with Avudaiyar-koil and the proper meaning of the term Ponnambalam.

I shall now procede to examine the 3rd, 6th and 7th of the seven grounds of Mr. Gopinatha Rao.

It is stated that the sage's name is not mentioned in any early inscription; and that the temple at Avudaiyar-Koil, which is comparatively new, does not contain any old inscription. Whether in the present state of South Indian epigraphy we should be justified in maintaining that because a historical personage is not mentioned in the inscriptions so far discovered, he cannot have lived earlier than those inscriptions is, to say the least, extremely doubtful; and any attempt to build an argument on such frail material is bound to be unsatisfactory. As regards the absence of old inscriptions on the walls of the temple at Avudaiyar-Koil, how can there be ancient inscriptions in a temple that is pronounced to be modern ?

Is it so certain that the identification of Tiru-Perum-Turai with Avudaiyar-Koil is correct? In spite of Mr. Gopinatha Row's emphatic statement I am inclined to hold that the identification is incorrect. Tiru-Perum-Turai means literally *Sacred-great-harbour*. In the earlier *Tiru Vilayadal Puranam* it is referred to as தாவுமா விறங்கு பட்டினம்; and Paranjothi Munivar describes it as வேலையந்துறை where steeds are landed and as கொட்புவி சார்தரு மாழ்கடலின்கரை where the Aryas landed their horses; and "Aryas" as seen from *Pingala-Nikandu* is synonymous with Mlechas. It is, therefore, necessary that the place to which Manikka Vacagar went for the purchase of horses should have been a sea-port town, that had trade with the Mlecha country. It was in such a town that the sage received his initiation. The Tiru

Vaçagam tells us that the town was in the "western land" and that it was girt with cocoanut groves; and in Paranjothi we read that in proceeding to Tiru-perum-turai, the sage crossed endless forests and mountain lands. The *Vatharurar Puranam* tells us that Manikka Vacagar made his way to the great Western harbour, through vast forests and over-interposing hills. The country described in the *Chilappadhikaram* is such a country, and it lies between Madura and the west coast. For the sea-port town to which our sage proceeded we should seek beyond these hills and forests and on the western coast. Mr. Ponnambalam Pillai identifies it with Tiru-puni-tura in Cochin; but Mr. Gopinatha Row says Tiru-puni-tura lay outside the Pandiyan kingdom, and so declines to accept the identification. I propose to identify the seat of Manikka Vacagar's conversion with VAIKAM in North Travancore. It cannot be said that it lay outside the Pandiyan kingdom, for the large lagoon on which the town of Vaikam borders is even now known by the name of *Vemba-nad* lake; and this points to the fact that the country round should originally have been Vemban or Pandiyan country. Vaikam is one of the most important Caiva shrines in Travancore; and the presiding Deity of the temple at Vaikam is now known as Perumtra-koil-Appan, which I beleive is only a corrupt rendering of Perum-turai-koil-Appan. Its principal festival is the Ashtami which is celebrated on the 8th lunar day of the dark-half of the month of Kartigai; and this festival, which is peculiar to this shrine, is according to tradition held in commemoration of Civan's manifestation on that day and in that place to a sage at the foot of a tree in the outer quadrangle of the temple. Though tradition says that the sage was Vyagrapadar, I believe the sage was not improbably Manikka Vacagar. The occurrence of such words as அச்சன் and எந்துவே and perhaps நின்னலை and பறை in the Tiruvacagam shows the influence of the present Malayalam country on Manikka Vacagar's language. There is also an ancient tradition that associates the name of Manikka Vacagar with a community known as Manigramakars who are even now found in Travancore and Cochin, and whose name appears in the Jewish grant. The Pandiyan kingdom had been founded many centuries before the Christian era; and Strabo speaks of an ambassador from the Pandiyan King to Augustus, which shows to what extent the foreign relations of the Pandiyan kingdom had then developed. At the time the Periplus (about 80 A. C.) the Pandiyan kingdom included the Malabar coast; and we know from the frequent mention of this country by classical writers, that the Pandiyan kingdom carried on in the centuries immediately before and after the Christian era a brisk trade with western nations. Vaikam also appears to have been, in the early centuries of the Christian era, a port to which foreign merchandise was brought. These considerations induce me to identify Tiru-perum-turai, the holy place where Manikka Vacagar met his Divine Guru, with Vaikam. It is not uncommon to find even now on both the east and the west coast places known by identical names and claiming identical sacred associations. In some instances, the town on the east coast lent its name and traditions to a newly created town in the west. In the present instance, I am inclined to believe that the town on the western coast had the honour of witnessing Manikka Vacagar's eventful conversion, and afterwards a counterpart of it in the eastern country was created, in the later generations of Caiva revival, and was invested with the sanctity and assigned the traditions that properly belonged to the town in the distant west. This will explain how, in the course of time, the new shrine in the east came to be so indissolubly associated with Manikka Vacagar. It may be mentioned that there is no trace or tradition of Avudaiyar-Koil having ever been a harbour nor is it in the 'western land.' The modernity of the temple at Avudaiyar Koil and the paucity of inscriptions cannot in the circumstances count for much; and these neither by themselves nor in conjunction with the grounds that have already been examined will be felt to be sufficiently strong or convincing to shake our faith in the accepted priority of Manikka Vacagar to the Devaram hymnists. Besides as we have seen, Tiru-perum-turai was already a shrine of repute in Appar's days.

The next contention is that because Manikka Vacagar refers to Chidambaram as Ponnambalam, he must have lived after Parantaka I. This is a common, but none the less a serious, error. It is conceded that Appar also refers to that renowned Caiva shrine by the same name; but as he has conclusively been proved to have lived in the seventh century, it will not do to say now that he too lived after Parantaka I, who belongs to the early years of the 10th century after Christ. So Mr. Gopinatha Row explains away the term in Appar as meaning only 'precious as gold,' but when the expression is employed by Manikka Vacagar it needs must denote 'made of gold', thus implying that the temple had already been gilded in his days. If that is true, we are assured our sage could not have lived before Parantaka I. We shall first glance at the lyrics in Appar where 'Ponnambalam' is employed to denote Chidambaram. It occurs in the fifth *Tirumurai*: we have there

1. செம்பொனம்பலத் துண்ணின்ற தாணுவை (Stanza 4.)
2. செம்பொனம்பலத் துண்ணின்ற அத்தனை (Stanza 5.)
3. சுடர்ச் செம்பொனி னம்பலத் தாதியை (Stanza 6.)
4. தூய செம்பொன்னினால்
   எழுதிமேய்ந்த சிற்றம்பலக் கூத்தனை. (Stanza 8.)

Mr. Gopinatha Row should have been in desperate straits indeed to urge that in these extracts "the way in which the appellation 'Ponnambalam' is used forces us to believe that Appar did not mean to describe it (Chidambaram) as actually 'made of gold,' but to indicate that it was as 'precious as gold'. Nevertheless the innocent word 'Ponnambalam' when used by Manikka Vacagar even by itself carries an entirely different meaning to his ears! There should be something strangely unnatural in one's modes of thought to make this possible. May we ask why the fiction of the temple at Chidambaram having been 'made of gold' should be still kept up by an acknowledged archaeologist? Besides, is it seriously contended that before Parantaka I Chidambaram was not known as Pon-Ambalam? Why should the testimony of literature be rejected in this matter? Umapathi Civachariya, the last of the canonized Caiva saints, who wrote his *Koil-Puranam* in the early years of the fourteenth century, ascribes the building of Ponnambalam to Hiraniya Varma who besides constructing the temple put a gold roof over it. Is it not posssible that long before Parantaka I, a remote ancester anticipated him as we are distinctly told in the *Koil-Puranam*? Or again, is it improbable that Parantaka only gilded the roof that the principal shrine of the Caivites—*the* Koyil or temple of Caiva sacred literature—which had from time immemorial been known as Ponnambalam—might justify its accepted or approved name? No further reason for this lavish display of munificence was needed for that pious and victorious prince than that the shrine had long been known as Pon-Ambalam. Perhaps Parantaka only imitated the act of his remote ancestor, just as we know for a fact that his own pious act was imitated afterwards; for we find Cekkilar, the prime-minister of Anapâya, who reigned in the latter half of the eleventh century, tells us that his patron also covered the roof of the shrine with gold.

The pious Nattukottai Chetties of to-day have covered the roof and wall with gilded plates because the shrine is known as Pon-Ambalam. Originally the chief shrine of the Caivites may have had the term Pon-Ambalam applied to it as merely an expresion of endearment, and subsequently the name may have realised itself by the munificent piety of of Hiraniya Varma or Parantaka. It is also possible that the temple came to be so called from the name of the Chola King Hiraniya Varma who built it. Certainly the appellation Pon-Ambalam in Manikka Vacagar does not and need not convey any reference to a temple built of gold. It was, however it originally arose, a term of endearment for the principal Caiva shrine, even as *Velli Ambalam* or 'silver hall' always denoted Madura. Even in the *Chilappathikaram* Madura is called by that name. Nobody has yet contended that Madura came to be known as 'Velli Ambalam' because any portion of the shrine there had been built of silver plates. We have such expression as அம்பொனுலவாய் in the Devaram and ஆடகமதுரை

in the Tiru Vacagam which will show in what sense 'golden' is employed. Besides Manikka Vacagar writes: கச்சித் திருவேகம்பன் செம்பொற்கோயிற்பாடி; and is it pretended to suggest that the temple at Kanchi was also built of or gilded with gold in the days of our sage. There is absolutely no warrant for holding that there is any thing in the manner in which Pon-Ambalam is employed by Manikka Vacagar that indicates that he refers to a gilded temple or a temple made of gold. Appar's line ஆய செம்பொன்னினொளியெழுதி மேய்ந்த சிற்றம்பலம் may bear that meaning; and if nevertheless it be felt that there can be no justification for placing him after Parantaka, I fail entirely to see how Manikka Vacagar can be brought after that Chola prince, simply because he uses the term பொன்னம்பலம். If Manikka Vacagar lived after Parantaka, it is, to say the least, highly inexplicable that he should make no reference whatever to that glorious prince even in his *Koil-Mutthu-Tiru-padigam,* which the sage sang standing before the very shrine that that monarch had covered with gold. Nambi Andar Nambi and Cekkilar are simply enthusiastic in singing his praises; and they came long after Manikka Vacagar. If his extraordinary munificence evoked such full-throated praise from these hagiographers who lived at least one or two centuries after that monarch, is it not natural to suppose that a devout Caiva poet appearing almost immediately after this great act, and singing the glories of the Divine Master to whom that monarch had shown such unique devotion, would, standing as he did in the very courtyard of the shrine that had benefited by this princely bounty, resound his praises with unstinted fervour and frequency? We are asked to believe that Manikka Vacagar appeared at just such a time, and yet there is not one single word in his lyrics about Parantaka. His silence can only mean that Parantaka and his gilding of the temple were unknown to him as they came only long after him; and that from the mere occurrence of Pon-Ambalam in the *Tiru Vacagam* we cannot jump to the conclusion that the sage lived after Parantaka Besides, it is clear that in his days Chidambaram had not become a Chola or even a Pallava shrine; for we find him referring to it as தென்னவனேற்றுஞ் சிற்றம்பலம்.

This leads us to the consideration of another statement made by Mr. Gopinatha Rao; and that relates to the mention of Varaguna by Manikka Vacagar. In his *Tiru-Chittambala Kovaiyar* or as it is usually called *Tiru Kovaiyar*, there are two references to Varaguna, and there is no doubt that the Varaguna that Manikka Vacagar mentions is the hero of the well-known *Tiru Vilaiyadal* where Civan satisfied with the exemplary devotion of the Pandiyan is pleased to bring down for his benefit Sivalokam from the heavens. This Varaguna is sought to be identified with a contemporary of the Ganga prince. Prithivipathi I, and if the identification is correct, the age of Varaguna, we are told would be about the first half of the ninth century; and as in the appendix to Mr. Seshagiri Sastriar's essay on 'Tamil literature' only one Varaguna is mentioned, Manikka Vacagar must have lived after the 9th century. To begin with, the Varaguna of Trichinopoly Rock-cave inscription even if he should be taken to denote a prince, does not appear to have been an independent monarch with any exceptional devotional or other merit deserving of specific mention by a great writer like Manikka Vacagar. The inscription is dated in the fourth year, 2501 st day of King Mâranjadayan; and it relates to a petty gift for the maintenance of four lamps, which if it is representative, is not the sort of munificence that would have merited or justified a special "sport" of Civan on his behalf which is found recorded in both the *Tiru Vilayadal Puranams*. Besides, Mr. Venkayya has shown from the Chinna-Mannur plates that there have been at least two Varagunas for whom archaeology can vouch; and this does not preclude the possibility but only strengthens the probability of other Varagunas before them. Thus the frail basis afforded by the appendix to Prof. Seshagiri Sastriar's essay for the identification is removed. The appeal, however, to Prof. Seshagiri Sastriar is misleading, for he gives only the list supplied by Paranjothi's *Tiru Vilayadal Puranam* which does not take us further than the seventh century after Chirist. I am prepared to grant that the legends of the *Tiru Vilayadal Puranam* are eminently unhistorical ; but the list of princes there given may, as observed by Mr. Wilson, be entitled to some confidence. "It is not unlikely, " writes that scholar in his introduction to the Descriptive Catalogue of the Mackenzie Collection, "that the compilers of the *Halasya Mahathmya* followed records reserved in the Madura temple and College, and have thus been able to give a tolerably regular and rational view of the series of kings". It has to be noted that the list of the Pandiyan Kings given in the *Tiru Vilayadal Puranam* and appended to Prof. Seshagiri Sastriar's essay ends with just one name after Kûn Pandiyan, the contemporary of Sambandâr, who lived in the 7th century. He is the 74th in the list, and Varaguna is the 19th. The Varaguna then of the *Tiru Vilayadal Puranam*, which may be accepted at least for determining the respective priority of the various Pandiyan princes known to Tamil Sacred Literature, cannot by any means have lived in the 9th century, but long anterior to the 7th century. The story of Varaguna whose devotional merit is extolled in Tamil literature is indissolubly associated with Tiru-Vidai-Maruthur, where as the *Tiru Vilayadal Puranam* tells us he lost his fell disease from which he had long suffered as the result of *Brahma Hatti.* When he entered the holy shrine at Tiru Vidai-Maruthur, Vembattur Nambi writes :

கீதிவாயிலினின்றது நீண்மதிற்புறத்தாக்
சேதமேதர வருந்திற லிரும்பிரமகத்தி

Now in Appar's lyrics relating to Tiru-Vidai-Maruthur we come across the following expressions :—

1. ஏதந்தீர்க்கு மிடைமருதா ;
2. பத்தர்க டங்கண் மேலை யேதங்க டீர நின்றார் ;
3. ஏதங்களான கடிவார் போலும் :

and in these descriptive phrases I believe we will be justified in recognising a reference to the release, by the grace of the God of Tiru-Vidai-Maruthur, from the

ஏதமேதர வருந்திற லிரும் பிரமகத்தி

that pursued Varaguna. The similarity in phraseology is so suggestive that the inference is almost irresistable. If so, we can with propriety hold that the legend associating Varaguna with Tiru-Vidai-Maruthur had become consecrated before Appar's days, and that therefore the Varaguna of Tamil literature was anterior to Appar, that is to the 7th century. It may be noticed here that it is not unusual for the Devaram hymnists to embody in their lyrics the traditions which legendary lore has particularly associated with the shrine in honour of which those lyrics are sung. Thus Tiru Jnana Sambandhar in singing of Kalahasti writes:

> வாய்சலசமாக வழிபாடு செய்யும் வேடன் மலராகு நயனங்
> காய்கணையினு லிடந்தீச னடிகூடு காளத்திமலையே.

Again, in singing of Mani-kuli, he writes:

> நித்த நியமத்தொழிலனாகி நெடுமால் குறளனாகி மிசவுஞ்
> சித்தம தொருக்கி வழிபாடு செயநின்ற சிவலோகனிடமாம்.

So too Appar in describing Tiru Vijaiya Mangai, sings:

> பாண்டுவின் மகன் பார்த்தன் பணி செய்து
> வேண்டு நல்வரங்கொள் விசையமங்கை.

I need not, however, multiply such instances. If I am correct in my surmise that Varaguna's providential cure from the effects of *Bramha Hatti* had become a consecrated legend even before Appar's days, then the Varaguna of the Trichinopoly inscription, serves only to throw us off the scent. Manikka Vacagar is expressly said to have lived in the days of Arimardhana Pandiyan whose minister he was. I confess I cannot understand why we should regard this Pandiyan as a 'mythical personage', simply because South Indian Epigraphy is as yet silent about him. We have various Kings and Chiefs mentioned in *Pura Nanuru*; and is it suggested that we should reject all of them as mythical just because their names have not been inscribed on stone? If we accepted the position that nothing that is not corroborated by epigraphical results is true, what would become of the history of the Tamil people at the beginning of the Christian era, not to go further back?

Epigraphy, so far as it goes, is one means of testing our results; but it is not the only means. And besides, the positive results of epigraphy alone have a value; not what it has left undone. To reason that because all kings mentioned in inscriptions have existed, and a particular king is not found to have been mentioned in inscriptions, therefore he did not exist, is to be guilty of an obvious logical fallacy. There is no reason so far as I can see at present to reject Arimarthana Pandiyan as a myth; and as already observed the list of princes supplied in the *Tiru Vilaiyadal Puranam* is entitled to confidence. At least it should not be rejected as a mere freak of imagination on mere *a priori* grounds, without conclusive evidence to show that it is false. Between Arimarthana Pandiyan who stands 61st in the list and Kun Pandiyan, 10 Pandiyans intervene; and if you assign to each of them the usual 25 years, then Arimarthana Pandiyan and therefore his minister Manikka Vacagar should be held to have lived 250 years before Kun Pandiyan. Kun Pandiyan was the contemporary of Sambandar who lived early in the 7th century. Thus we will have to seek for Manikka Vacagar in the latter half of the 4th century.

V. Conclusion.

This is the conclusion I had arrived at elsewhere, though on other grounds. It is well-known that Pêrasiriyar, one of the earliest commentators in Tamil, has written an elaborate commentary on Manikka Vacagar's *Tiru–Koviyar.* The date of Pêrasiriyar will supply the lower limit for the age of Manikka Vacagar. Mr. Anavarathanayagam Pillai M. A., in his learned paper on Nachinarkkiniyar that appeared in the *Madras Christian College Magazine*, has shown that Pêrasiriyar should be sought for in the latter part of the 7th or probably in the early part of the 8th century after Christ. Perasiriyar came after Appar as he cites an illustration in his commentary from one of Appar's hymns. The difference in treatment accorded to the works of the two saints by the commentator will form a good index to the respective distance of time between him and them. Manikka Vacagar's work had by that time become invested with sufficient importance and sanctity to deserve an erudite commentary; while only a stray passage from the earliest of the Devaram hymnists is utilised as an illustration by the commentator. This would indicate that Manikka Vacagar preceded Appar. In the *Devâram* hymns are found expressions and passages that remind one forcibly of the language of the *Tiru Vacagam.* A few illustrative parallel passages will suffice. Thus we may note the following:

1. *சிந்தையே கோயிற்கொண்ட வெம்பெருமான்*

and *அறவையேன் மனமே கோயிலாக்கொண்டு—Manikka Vacagar.*

நினைப்பவர் மனங்கோயிலாக்கொண்டவன் —*Appar.*

2. *யாவர்கோன் என்னையும்வந் தாண்டுகொண்டான்*

யாமார்க்கும் குடியல்லோம் யாது மஞ்சோம்–Manikka Vacagar.

விடையான் விரும்பியென் னுள்ளத் திருந்தனனினி நமக்கிங்

கடையா வவல மருவினைசாரா நமனையஞ்சோம்

and *நாமார்க்குங் குடியல்லோம் நமனையஞ்சோம்.* —*Appar.*

3. விச்சதன்றியே விளைவு செய்குவாய் —*Manikka Vacagar*

விச்சின்றி நாறு செய்வான் —*Appar.*

4. தடக்கையின் நெல்லிக்கனி யெனக்காயினன்-*Manikka Vacagar.*

கையிலாமலகக்கனி யொக்குமே —*Appar.*

5 பூங்கமலத் தயனொடு மாலறியாத —*Manikka Vacagar.*

அங்கமலத் தயனொடு மாலுங்காணா —*Appar.*

Parallel passages from the other *Devaram* hymnists may also be cited; but there is no necessity; for if it be shown, as it is morally held, that Manikka Vacagar's influence is perceptible in Appar's fervent lyrics, then Manikka Vacagar must perforce have lived long anterior to all the *Devaram* writers. The orthodox view that Manikka Vacagar preceded Appar is not merely fanciful; for Appar definitely refers to our sage. I have tried to show that in one of Appar's Tiru-Arur hymns there is a distinct reference to a miracle which tradition has always associated with only one historical personage, viz., Manikka Vacagar; and this reference shows that by the time of Tiru Navukku Arasu a halo of sanctity had settled round the name and life of Manikka Vacagar. It appears to me that Appar makes other references too to Manikka Vacagar. In the 6th *Tiru Murai*, he sings:

1. கீதத்தை மிகப்பாடு மடியார்க்கென்றுங் கேடிலாவானுலகங் கொடுத்த [நாளோ.

2. மறம்பலவுமுடையாரை மயக்கந்தீர்த்து மாமுனிவர்க் கருள்செய் [தங்கிருந்த நாளோ.

3. பலவாயவேடங்கடானேயாகிப் பணிவார்கட்கங்கங்கேபற்றானானை.

4 மலங்கெடுத்து மாதீர்த்த மாட்டிக்கொண்ட மறையவனை

and in these lines I am inclined to hold that Appar refers to our sage's conversion. We learn from the Tiru Vacagam that our sage was taught the mystery of emancipating grace by Civan in the guise of Brahmin Guru seated "by Perumthurai's pleasant lake beneath the *Kurunthum's* flowery shade." The most conclusive reference, however, to Manikka Vacagar is found in one of Appar's *Tiru Thândagam* in the 6th *Tiru Murai*, where our saint is specifically mentioned. The passage I refer to is குடமுழ நந்தீசனை வாசகனாக்கொண்டார். In this passage, Appar expressly speaks of Vaçagan வாசகர் or Manikka Vacagar, and the traditional belief that Manikka Vacagar is an incarnation of Nandhi is also expressly stated in this passage. We have the authority of the greatest living Tamil scholar of South India, Mahamahopadhiyaya Pandit V. Swaminatha Iyer of the Madras Presidency College for this view. This passage clinches the question we are now considering; and after this significant passage in Appar's தனித்திருத்தாண்டகம் there cannot be the slightest shadow of a doubt that Manikka Vacagar preceded Appar. By the time of Appar, Manikka Vacagar had attained such high sanctity as to justify the former's unqestioning faith in the tradition regarding Manikka Vacagar as an incarnation of Nandhi. It is reasonable to conclude, therefore, that Manikka Vacagar preceded Appar by at least a century or two; and if Appar is to be sought for at the close of the sixth or the beginning of the seventh century, we will have to go to a period not later than the close of the fourth century for Manikka Vacagar. The priority of our sage to Appar, the earliest of the Devaram hymnists, may also be domonstrated by a comparison of the forms of metre adopted by the two poets. Manikka Vacagar employs the *Agaval* and the *Venba* forms, which are the characteristic metres of the old Sangam authors, as also the Virutham metre so common and so well developed in later writers. The Devaram hymnists, including Appar, have written mainly in the latter form. Thus having regard to the form of the *Tiru Vacagam* lyrics, Manikka Vacagar marks the transition from the old Sangam writers to the later poets and it is partly on this ground that Pandit *Vedachalam* Pillai of the Christian College, Madras, places our sage in the 3rd century A. C.

Other facts may also be gathered from Tamil literature to show that Manikka Vacagar should have lived long prior to Appar. We find imitations of Manikka Vacagar's lyrics in the writings of the Vaishnava Alwars. Our sage's *Tiru châlal* (திருச்சாழல்) and *Kôttumbi* (கோத்தும்பி) have afforded models for similar songs by Tiru Mangai Mannan. From Tiru Mangai Alwar's works we find that he was a contemporary of Vaira Meghan, who has been shown to belong to the 8th century.* There is also a tradition current among the Vaishnavas that Tiru Mangai Mannan had a successful disputation with Tiru Jnana Sambandar, and the tradition is supported by Pinbazhakia Manavâla Jîyar in his *Guru Paramparai.* If this be believed, Tiru Mangai Alwar should be taken to have lived in the 7th century. Mr. S. Krishnaswamy Iyengar of Bangalore has, in a learned paper that he contributed to the Indian Antiquary, shown that Tiru Mangai Alwar should be sought for in the first half of the 8th century, and that he was a younger contemporary of Jnana Sambandar.† It will not be doubted by any body that this last of the Alwars lived several centuries after Manikka Vacagar; and we have the authority of Mr. Gopinatha Rao himself for holding that even Nammalwar, the sixth of the Vaishnava Alwars came only after our sage. We find from *Tiru Mangai* Alwar's *Periya Tiru Moli* that in his days Chidambaram had not become a Chola possession, but continued to be in the hands of the Pallavas. From this it is clear that the Vaishnava saint, and *a fortiori* Manikka Vacagar, should have lived long before Parantaka Chola. Again Manikka Vacagar's *Tiru-Palli-Eluchi* (திருப் பள்ளி யெழுச்சி) has induced a similar lyric by Thondar Adi Podi Alwar; and this Alwar according to tradition lived about a century before Tiru Mangai Mannan. If Tiru Mangai Alwar and Thondar Adi Podi Alwar enable us to place Manikka Vacagar anterior to the 7th or even to the 6th century, a reference to Andal and Nammalwar enables us to take our sage further back.

---

* *Sen-Tamil* Vol I. p. 232.

† Vide Prof. Krishnasami Aiyengar's "Tiru Mangai Alwar and his date" in Indian Antiquary, XXXV; and Pandit Ragava Aiyengar's articles in Sen-Tamil III and IV.

His *Kuyil Decad* and *Tiru Pâvai* have suggested similar lyrics by Andal in honor of Sri Krishna. It may be noted that there is similarity not only in the refrains and the metre and rythm employed by the Caiva and Vaishnava bards, but also not infrequently in the very expressions employed and the ideas conveyed by them; and this parallelism exists in the case of other lyrics of Manikka Vacagar and their Vaishnava counterparts by Tiru Mangai Mannan and Thondar Adi Podi Alwar mentioned above. By way of illustration we may just glance at the *Maidens' Reville* (திருப் பாவை) by Manikka Vacagar and by Andal. Both poems are written in the same metre இயற்றரவிணை கொச்சகக் கலிப்பா; and the refrain in both, எலோர் எம்பாவாய், is the same. They are both impassioned calls to maidens and matrons who symbolise the human soul—to rise before dawn from their sleep (of darkness) in the month of Margaly—which marks the beginning of evolution and activity in nature that they may bathe betimes in the refreshing waters of life and grace.

போற்றியா மார்கழி நீராடேலோ ரெம்பாவாய்—*Tiru Vacagam,*

மார்கழித் திங்கள் மதி நிறைந்த நன்னாளால்
நீராடப்போதுவீர் போதுமினோ நேரிழையீர்.—*Andal's.*

It is the custom even to-day among at least orthodox Brahmins of both sexes in Southern India, whether they be Smarthas or Vaishnavas, to have their morning bath before dawn throughout Margali, so that they may finish their worship and glorification of God by sun rise. Reading these songs together, one is certain to be struck by the great similarity in words and ideas that exists between them. To note a few instances:

In the Tiru Vacagam we have:

—அரும் பெருஞ்
சோதியையாம் பாடக்கேட்டேயும் வாட்டடங்கண்
மாதே! வளருதியோ?

In Andal we read:

நாயகப் பெண்பிள்ளாய் நாராயணன்மூர்த்தி
கேசவனைபபாடவும் நீ கேட்டே கிடத்தியோ!

Again in Manikka Vacagar occur the following lines:—

> கோழி சிலம்பச் சிலம்புங் குருகெங்கு
> மேழி லியம்ப இயம்பும் வெண் சங்கெங்கும்

and with these may be compared the following from Andal:

> புள்ளுஞ் சிலம்பினகாண் புள்ளரையன்கோயிலில்
> வெள்ளை விளிசங்கின் பேரரவங்கேட்டிலையோ

Yet again with the following from the *Tiru Vacagam*

> கேழில் பரஞ்சோதி கேழில் பரங்கருணை
> கேழில் விழுப்பொருள்கள் பாடினேங் கேட்டிலையோ!
> வாழி யீதென்ன? உறக்கமோ வாய்திறவாய்!

may be compared

> மனத்துக் கினியானைப்பாடவும் நீ வாய்திறவாய்
> இனித்தானெழுந்திரா யீதென்ன பேருறக்கம்,

from Andal.

So again the *Tiru Vacagam* has

> ஒண்ணித்தில நகையாய் இன்னம் புலர்ந்தின்றோ?
> வண்ணக் கனிமொழியார் எல்லாரும் வந்தாரோ?

and these lines find a reflection in Andal's poem where we have

> எல்லே யிளங்கிளியே யின்னமுறங்குதியோ
> எல்லாரும் போந்தாரோ போந்தார் போந்தெண்ணிக்கொள்.

Just one more parellel. In Manikka Vacagar we read

> மானே நீ நென்னலை நாளைவந் துங்களை
> நானே யெழுப்புவன் என்றலு நாணாமே
> போன திசை பகராய் இன்னம் புலர்ந்தின்றோ.

and its paraphrase in Andal is as follows:—

> எங்களை முன்ன மெழுப்புவான் வாய்பேசும்
> நங்கா யெழுந்திராய் நாணாதாய் நாவுடையாய்.

Turning to Nammalwar, there can be no doubt that the name *Tiruvâymoli* (திருவாய்மொழி) by which his principal work is known, was suggested by the name of Manikka Vacagar's great work, the *Tiru Vacagam*. Nammalwar's *Tiru Viruthum*, (திருவிருத்தம்) another well-known work is obviously the Vaishnava analogue to Manikka Vacagar's *Tiru Koraiyar* (திருக் கோவையார்) in the department of *Agapporul*. In these two works of Nammalvar we find echoes from Manikka Vacagar. The fifth stanza of the 8th *Tiru-vaymoli* of the *Ettâmpâttu* is as follows:—

நின்ற வொன்றை யுணர்ந்தேனுக்கதனுள் நேர்மை யது விதுவென்று
ஒன்று மொருவர்க்குணரலாகா துணர்ந்து மேலுங் காண்பரிது
சென்று சென்று பரம்பரமாய் யாதுமின்றித் தேய்ந்தற்று
நன்று தீதென் றறிவரிதாய் நன்றாய் ஞானங் கடந்ததே;

and it can be easily seen that we have here a remarkable adaptation, if not an exact reproduction of the words and ideas in Manikka Vacagar's *Koil-Tiru-Padigam*.

இன்றெனக் கருளி இருள்கடிந் துள்ளத்
தெழுகின்ற ஞாயிறே போன்று
நின்றநின் றன்மை நினைப்பற நினைந்தே
னீயலாற் பிறிதுமற் றின்மை
சென்றுசென் றணுவாய்த் தேய்ந்துதேய்ந் தொன்றாந்
திருப்பெருந் துறையுறை சிவனே
ஒன்றுநீ யல்லை அன்றியொன் றில்லை
ஆருன்னை யறியகிற் பாரே. *Tiru Vacagam* 22—7.

In stanza 94 of *Tiru Viruthum*, Nammalwar writes:

எப்படி யூரா மிலைக்கக் குருட்டா மிலைக்கு மென்று
மப்படி யானுஞ் சொன்னே னடியேன் மற்றியா தென்பனே.

and here we have a reproduction not merely of ideas but even of the very words employed by Manikka Vacagar, who in stanza 87 of his *Tiru Chathagam* (திருச் சதகம்) says:

ஊராமிலைக்கச் குருட்டா மிலைத்திங் குன்றாளிணை யன்புக்
காராவடியே னயலே மயல்கொண் டழுகேனே.

Other instances of parallelism between our sage and Nammâlwâr may be cited; but these will suffice. I am not aware that any body has claimed that Nammalwar preceded Manikka Vacagar. A comparison of their work will convince any one that Manikka Vacagar was the earlier of the two. The language and metre of Nammalwar's poem and the plan and arrangement of his lyrics suggest proximity more to the days of the earlier Devaram hymnists than to the period of transition from the old Sangam writers to these later bards, to which Manikka Vacagar clearly belongs to. There can be no doubt that the line in the *Tiru Viruthcam* is a quotation from Manikka Vacagar, and the lines from the *Tiru Vâymoli* quoted above are a startling echo of Manikka Vacagar's words. When did Nammalwar live? The great master singer of Tamil Epic poetry, Kamban, refers to Nammalwar in his *Sadagopar Anthathi* as சுருதிப்பொருக்கும் ஆயிரம் பா பண்ணி செய்தவரே; thus showing that there was a very long distance of time between the sage and the poet. I am not aware that any sound argument has yet been advanced to discredit the traditional Saka 807 or 885 A. C. assigned to Kamban's Ramayanam. Nammalwar must, therefore, have lived long before the 9th century to justify his deification by Kamban. Admittedly Nammalwar was anterior in date to Perialwar; and Perialwar, as his works show, was a contemporary of Nedumaran, the victor of *Nêlveli*. Nelvêli-venra-ninra-çîr-Nedu-Mâran is the well-known Kûn Pandiyan, the contemporary of Tiru Jnana Sambandar. Perialwar, therefore, belonged to the 7th century and Nammalwar should be sought for prior to that date. Tiru Mangai Alwar who came within a century of Perialwar arranged for the public worship of Nammalwar and the recital of his *Tiruvaymoli* in Sri-Rangam. In order that Nammalwar might be accorded the dignity of a saint in Sri-Rangam itself in the days of Tiru Mangai Mannan, that sage should have flourished at least two centuries before he acquired such dignity; and thus we will not be wrong in seeking for Nammalwar about 450 or 500 A.C. I am emboldened in this conclusion by the knowledge that Professor Krishnaswamy Aiyengar, M. A., of Bangalore is also of a similar view.* Thus then, we arrive

* The Madras Christian College Magazine April 1904.

at the conclusion that Manikka Vacagar should be sought for before the middle of the 5th century. Even if you allow only a difference of 50 years between Manikka Vacagar and Nammalwar–and it will be conceded that 50 years is a very modest demand in the circumstances–we easily arrive at the date which I consider is the latest that can be assigned to Manikka Vacagar, and that is the last quarter of the 4th century after Christ.

I have so far attempted in this paper to establish that orthodox view, which places Manikka Vacagar several centuries before the Devaram hymnists, is fully supported by the evidence afforded by Tamil litrature itself, and that there are specific references to Manikka Vacagar in the Devaram lyrics. By more than one process I have also attempted to show that the lower limit for the age of Manikka Vacagar is afforded by the last quarter of the 4th century of the Christian era; and I am proud to acknowledge that the late Dr. Pope had shortly before his death expressed in one of his letters that he was content to accept this conclusion. Perhaps Manikka Vacagar lived before the 4th century; but certainly not later. Tradition says that Manikka Vacagar had a disputation with the Ceylon Buddhists, which resulted in the conversion to Caivism of the daughter of the King of Ceylon; and it is popularly believed that this contest is embodied in the sage's *Tiru-Châlal*. The *Mahavansa* relates a religious controversy in the 3rd century after Christ which almost entirely answers to this tradition. That chronicle says that in the reign of Gothabhaya alias Mêghavarnabhaya (254 to 267 A.C a .) Tamil priest from the Chola country, profoundly versed in the rites of the *Bhuta* or Demon faith had a disputation with the *Thera* of the Sangabalaparivena, and succeeded in overcoming the tenets of the latter, with the consequence that he completely gained the confidence of the King of Ceylon, who placed his younger son under his tuition. In the legend connected with Manikka Vacagar, it is the daughter of the King of Ceylon that is said to have been converted, while in the chronicle it is the son: but otherwise the confirmation afforded by the *Mahavansa* to the tradition described in the *Vatha Urar Puranam* is almost convincing. If my conjecture is correct that the two accounts refer really to the same fact or occurrence, we will be justified in assigning Manikka Vacagar to the 2nd and 3rd quarters of the 3rd century after Christ. The time has not yet arrived when one can afford to be positive on a point of South Indian chronology; nevertheless one may be reasonably certain that Manikka Vacagar was long anterior to Appar, the earliest of the Devaram hymnists, and his probable date is the 3rd and certainly not later than the 4th century of the Christian era. I have attempted to establish this from such data as are now available; and if in this attempt I have succeeded, then one important date in the history of Tamil literature may be regarded as fairly settled; and we may, in spite of certain recent attempts to make out the contrary, still hold, not merely as a pious sentiment, but with good reason and legitimate pride, that our literature is really ancient.

Manikka Vaçagar

AND THE

Early Christians of Malabar.

BY

T. Ponnambalam Pillai Esq., M. R. A. S.

In his interesting work entitled *Christianity in Travancore*, Mr. G. T. Mackenzie, the British Resident in the Courts of Travancore and Cochin, makes a very brief mention of the visit of the Tamil sage Manikka Vacagar to Malabar and of the reconversion of some early Syrian Christians to Hinduism. The literature on the subject is so very scanty that we thought that it would be of some interest to the general readers to have some details which, however, are not easy to obtain. Though European *savants* have traced the visit of the Tamil saint to Malabar, yet this piece of information is not generally known to those who devour with avidity the soul-stirring and melodious hymns of Manikka Vacagar. Some of the learned priests and dignitaries of the Syrian Church in Travancore seem to have a fund of information on the subject, but many of them could not or would not place the materials that they have at our disposal. The descendants of the *Manigramakars* from whom much valuable information can be gleaned seem to be chary of furnishing us with any facts which would tend to throw light on their past history, probably under the mistaken impression that they would be ostracised from the Hindu society. The work of unfolding the connection of Manikka Vacagar with the early Christians of Malabar is therefore not a very easy one. With the scanty materials which we have been able to collect we shall try to reconstruct the story of the readmission of a few Christians into the Hindu fold.

The discussion of the subject may be begun by giving an account of the life of the sage as related in the *Vathavur* and *Thiruvilaiyadal* puranams. The latter is termed in Sanskrit, *Halasya Mahatmyam* by which name it goes in this part of Southern India. The former is supposed to contain an account of his life, while *Thiruvilaiyadal* deals only with two important incidents in his life. These works are not of great historical value. The chief events connected with the life of Manikka Vacagar were handed down from generation to generation till they were shrouded in a halo of romance. Kadavul Mâ-Muni, the author of the *Va'havur* puranam, took them up at that point and clothed them in Tamil metre. From the diction employed in it, it is evident that it is of recent origin. The portions referring to the saint in the *Thiruvilaiyadal* puranam differ slightly from the version given in the other. Though these are not trustworthy records of the life of the saint, still there is a substratum of truth in them.

The sage was born of humble, but respectable and pious Brahman parents of Tiru Vathavur on the banks of the Vaigai and named after that place. He was of such a precocious intellect that he soon mastered all the *Vedas*, *Agamas* and other studies prescribed for an orthodox Brahman. The austere life led by one so young and the consummate knowledge he had acquired in all branches of learning within a short period, attracted the notice of Arimarthanan, the then reigning Pandiyan. He invited him to his Court and treated him with great consideration. When he found out his worth and was satisfied of what mettle he was made, he appointed him to the high office of Prime Minister under the title of Tennavan Pirama Rayan, meaning the Brahman minister of the Southern King, though he was only in his teens.

Though the young minister was all-powerful in the State his head was not turned. He knew that the external lustre with which he was surrounded was worthless. In the midst of the task he had to perform with tact, skill and impartiality as the chief minister of an important kingdom, he was always intent on the emancipation of his soul, and the working of the salvation of the thronging multitude, who were rushing headlong towards perdition. Thus, in the midst of his arduous temporal duties, he always found time to study the sacred writings connected with the *Caiva Siddhanta* philosophy, to hold discussions with those learned in them, and to contemplate upon the infinite grace of the Supreme Being. As years rolled on in this manner, it struck him that he could not attain the end he had in view without a guide, and he longed to secure his *Guru.*

While the process of transformation of the mind of the sage was thus gradually proceeding, it so happened that on a certain day when the Pandiyan was sitting in state, surrounded with all oriental pomp, some messengers announced to him the arrival of a large number of horses in a great harbour in the Chola kingdom. In view of strengthening his cavalry, the King commanded the Prime Minister to go to Tiru-perum-turay and purchase all the available horses for him. For this purpose Arimarthanan furnished him with the necessary funds and a magnificient escort which made Manikka Vacagar move in great state. After going through crowded cities, vast forests and forest-clad hills, he reached his destination.

Lo! what did he espy at Tiru-perum-turay—the great sacred harbour? When he approached a beautiful grove filled with ever-green trees, whose flowers were emitting sweet fragrance and where the bees were humming their honeyed songs and birds of plumage were filling the air with their melodies from every branch, he heard the chanting of the *Agamas.* He stopped his cavalcade and despatched some messengers to ascertain where the music came from. They returned and informed him that they saw a sage with garlands of Cassia flowers round his head resembling the great Civa himself, sitting under the shade of a *Kurumta* tree *(Trichilia)* surrounded by a host of disciples. On this, Manikka Vacagar thought to himself that the *Guru* whom he had long been seeking had come and that his salvation was not far off. He went into the sacred grove unattended, found his guide who welcomed him and initiated him into the mysteries of the *Caiva Siddhanta* philosophy. Thenceforward he became absorbed in devotion and incessantly expressed his feelings of gratitude to God for having made him his own, and for having paved his way for his beatitude. For, it was God that revealed himself to him and became his *Guru*. Having assumed the life of an ascetic under instructions from him, Manikka Vacagar parted with all that he had, including the enormous treasure belonging to the King and the rich garments in which he was robed.

His relations and other members of the escort who accompanied Manikka Vacagar, observing all that had taken place, approached him with all respect, and remonstrated with him gently that it was improper not to think of carrying out the object of the mission on which he had repaired to the place, and thus to incur the displeasure of the King. But the sage sternly bade them quit his presence and said that he would have nothing to do with anything that was not spiritual. Being disappointed that their expostulations were not of any avail, they wended their way to Madura, and informed the King of all that had transpired. The enraged Pandiyan caused the following epistle couched in sarcastic terms to be prepared and put into the hands of the nimblest of his messengers to be delivered to Manikka Vacagar:

From

THE KING PANDIYAN.

To

THE GOOD MINISTER.

Thennavan Pirama Royan.

"It has amused us to learn that having squandered the boundless "treasure taken from us, you have thought it proper to assume the garb of "an ascetic instead of making purchases of horses for us. We have also "been impressed with the results of your learning which bid you beg from "door to door, impelled by bodily appetites, giving up the splendours of a "Court life, and to consider that it is profitable to prove treacherous to the "sovereign who was proved your benefactor. In case you think that to "deal with earthly kings is to associate with reptiles that emit venom, we "command you to return forthwith to this city on receipt of this message."

When the letter was put into the hands of Manikka Vacagar, he thought to himself that he could be the servant only of the servants of Civa and that the Pandiyan had no business to say that he was his sovereign, and said to himself that even the messengers of the God of Death dared not approach him. In this state of mind he laid the letter before the Guru who smiled at it, and bade him return fearlessly and inform the King that the horses would be at Madura on the 19th of Avany during the hours of the *mûlam* star. God Civa, further assured Manikka Vacagar that he himself would take them, and they would be of such a breed that their fame would resound throughout the kingdom. At the same time he furnished him with such garments, jewels and vehicles as became the minister of the Crown. Civa also handed over to him a rare ruby that it might be presented to the King.

Accordingly, Manikka Vacagar returned with the messengers, waited upon the Pandiyan, made the usual obeisance reluctantly, and presented him with the ruby above referred to. The King looked at it over and over again with great delight and astonishment, requested Manikka Vacagar to seat himself down and relate all that had taken place. He submitted as follows: "I took the large sum of money, Your " Majesty was pleased to hand over to me, selected and " purchased the most sound and best trained horses; next I " consulted the Brahman astrologers for a suitable date to " take them to Madura, and they fixed the 19th of Avany " under the *Mûlam* star. On this, I tarried at Tiru-perum- " turai, but your Majesty's Staff Officers were impatient to " return. Owing to their misrepresentations, Your Majesty " was pleased to write an angry letter which made me return " at once. The horses will be brought here on the day named " by me." The King was satisfied with the explanation of the Minister and assured him of his unabated confidence. Requesting him not to mind the contents of the letter, he took him to his Palace, loaded him with jewels and clothes of honour, and desired him to repair to his residence, and look after the duties of his office.

Some days before the expected arrival of the steeds, an Under-Secretary of State gained the ears of the Pandiyan King and made him understand that the story of the expected arrival of horses was a fabrication, that the money which Manikka Vacagar had taken was handed over to a person who put on the guise of a great *Guru*, that nothing was done in the way of purchasing horses and that they were not stabled at Tiru-perum-turai, as was reported by the Prime Minister. On this, the King despatched messengers to repair to the place and verify the statement of Manikka Vacagar. They performed the object of their mission and intimated to the King the fruitlessness of their searches which extended all over the great sacred harbour and other cities. On this, the Pandiyan became enraged and ordered the imprisonment of the sage, which naturally caused him to lament over his fate, and invoke the protection of Civa. On the following morning, the King performed his usual ablutions, sat in the portico of his palace and called upon the myrmidons of Justice, to compel Manikka Vacagar to disgorge the fabulous treasure he had misspent under the pretence of purchasing horses for him. While the process of administering justice by placing the saint in an inconvenient posture with his face up turned towards the scorching sun, and subjecting him to other indignities was going on, the sky was darkened by a cloud of dust and the air was filled with the clanging of iron-shod hoofs and the neighing of "prancing palfreys." On enquiry it was found that the expected horses were on their way to Madura. At last, they arrived. The King saw how he had wronged his Minister. He at once ordered his release, and took him with him to view the cavalcade which was led by noble Arab. The Pandiyan was mightily pleased with what he saw and directed his minister to request the chief of the horse dealers to pass the horses through all the evolutions in which they had been practised, and the King's commands were obeyed. He ordered dresses of honour to be bestowed on the Arabs which they received on the end of their whips. This no doubt irritated the King, but his Minister explained the apparent contempt as the outcome of their native custom. Satisfied with the explanation, he requested the Arabs to explain to him the nature of the marks of horses and their effects on man, and they accordingly instructed him on the points. The only business that remained to be transacted was the delivery of the horses, which was done by the formal exchange of ropes between the King's grooms and the Arabs. Having convinced the King that they had supplied him with horses for eight times the value paid by Manikka Vacagar, they took their departure. After they were stabled, the King and his minister retired to their Palaces. During night the town was filled with frightful howlings. The new comers turned into jackals in the dead of night, fell upon the real horses that had been stabled there, killed most of them and escaped into the adjacent jungles. The truth was that when Civa heard of the sufferings of his faithful adherent, he collected a vast multitude of foxes, metamorphosed them into magnificent steeds, put them in charge of the celestials as syces, and himself assuming the guise of a wealthy Arab merchant, commanded the cavalcade. The enraged King sent for his minister, upbraided him for the trick he had played on him and handed him over to the agents of torture to wring out the enormous sum of money he had deprived him of. The tormentors took him to the burning sand on the bed of the river Vaigai, exposed him to the fierce noontide sun, and placed a huge stone on his back.

In all his difficulties, Manikka Vacagar, always turned to God and prayed fervently to grant him relief. This occasion was no exception to the rule. God Civa heard his pathetic prayers and sent down the waters of the Ganges from his bushy locks into the Vaigai. They overflew its banks and threatened to destroy the Pandiyan capital. The King was bewildered, and his equally astonished ministers advised him to restore the sage to his liberty as the floods were the result of the wrath of God provoked by the ill-treatment to which he was subjected. The Pandiyan was of the same view. He at once restored Manikka Vacagar to his favour and charged him with the duty of saving his metropolis. The very first thing the sage did was to pray for the subsidence of the flood. The next thing the reinstated Prime Minister did was to call upon the citizens to throw up dams on both the banks of the river and allotted a portion of the work to each citizen. A very small portion of the work fell to the share of a poor widow, by name Cem-mana-Celvi who eked out her existence by baking and selling a rice cake known by the designation of *Puttu*. The poor woman was at her wits' end. For, she had no male member in the family to assist her, and she could command no funds to employ labour. Even if she was able to pay, she could procure no labourers as every individual in the town was engaged on his own behalf. At such a juncture all that she was able to do was to offer prayers to God, and He heard her. The result was the appearance of a rustic youth clad in rags with a basket on his head and spade on his shoulders. In this garb, he cried out if there were people to engage his services. The old lady was beside herself with joy at the sudden appearance of cooly, and at once she bargained with him. He demanded his wages in advance, but she pleaded her inability to comply with that condition. Nevertheless, she offered to recompense him at the close of the day after selling her cakes, or if he was particular about the advance she expressed her willingness to give him some cakes. He accepted the latter term, got a quantity of the crumblings of the cake, tied it fast to one end of his tattered clothes and set to work to finish the portion allotted to Cem-mana-Celvi. But he was more mindful of devouring the poor woman's cakes than completing the portion assigned to him, and thus relieving her of her responsibility. He would now and then throw a basketful or two of earth at the appointed place, wash down the crumbled cake with the water of the Vaigai, dance about, sing and sleep. When the old lady appealed to him, he assured her of his determination to finish his work, and to have no misgivings about it, and even prevailed on her to return home. The officers of the King who were superintending the work found that every one except this cooly had done his work satisfactorily. As he was a defaulter who deserved condign punishment, one of the officers asked him to appear before his immediate superior, but he refused to do so. On this he was taken by force. On questioning him he offered no explanation, and he was therefore ordered to be mercilessly flogged. With the first blow, the cooly vanished, and the whole universe received the stroke. Then it was patent that God himself came in the disguise of a day-labourer, in order to demonstrate to the world the piety of Manikka Vacagar. By this time the King knew all, and offered to resign his crown in his favour. But the saint had only one wish. It was to be divested of all mundane cares that he might devote all his time to the service of his God Civa. The Pandiyan readily acceded to his wishes and relieved him of all his responsibilities.

On this, he again assumed the garb of an ascetic and followed the bent of his will. The first thing he did was to proceed to Tiru-perum-turay and pay his obeisance to his *Guru*. He spent a considerable time there and composed no fewer than twenty of his hymns. The next event in the life of the sage was his pilgrimage to sacred shrines. He began it with Uttara Kosa Mangai, seven miles from Ramnad, and ended with Chidambaram. Most of the remaining hymns were composed during these visits, and the last mentioned place contributed the largest number. Finding that he had seen enough of the Chola and Pandiyan kingdoms, he was anxious to visit Ceylon. At that time Buddhism was the prevailing religion of that Island, and it was also the one supported by the State. Manikka Vacagar proceeded to Ceylon and wandered all over the place muttering always something about Ponnambalam or Golden Porch. The professors of Buddhism thought it rather strange that an ascetic with his bowl and staff should always be muttering in the way he did. The intelligence was conveyed to the King who sent for Manikka Vacagar. He at first declined to go as he had nothing to do with earthly sovereigns. But at last he stood before him and his chief priest. The latter put Manikka Vacagar a number of insulting questions and then vowed he would go to Chidambaram, enter into a disputation with the Hindu votaries there, establish that Buddha was the only God, and the Golden Porch was his shrine. In fulfilment of his vow the chief priest left for Southern India followed by the king who took his tributary presents to his paramount Lord Chola. Manikka Vacagar having attained the object of his mission also left the place and returned to Tillai.

On his arrival at Chidambaram, the Buddhist chief priest went direct into the sacred edifice and took up his residence there. When the servants of the temple remonstrated with him and called upon him to quit it, he said that he would not do so till he had vanquished the followers of Civa in a disputation held in the presence of the Chola King and established the image of Buddha in the Golden Porch. The matter was communicated to the 2,999 Brahmans of the place, and on their repeating the remonstrance, they also received the same curt and discourteous reply. On this, the Chola King was summoned with all the learned men in the land, and a day was appointed for the discussion. The name of Manikka Vacagar who was living in the suburbs of the city was in a supernatural manner suggested as the proper person to lead the followers of Civa, and he gladly undertook to uphold the cause of Hinduism. The day arrived, and the conference was held in the hall occupied by the Buddhists. It was literally packed as pious Brahmans and other devotees from every part of the country thronged to the place. The Kings, of Chola and Ealam (Ceylon) were in the assembly. The latter was there with his dumb daughter. Manikka Vacagar began the contest, and after a hot debate, it came to an end, and the Buddhist priests were dumfounded. The victory was complete. The King of Ceylon prostrated himself before Manikka Vacagar and confessed his conversion to the tenets of Caiva Siddhanta philosophy, and begged him to give his daughter the power of speech. The prayer was heard. Soon after this, the discomfitted monks renounced their religion, smeared themselves with sacred ashes, put on rosaries of *Eleocarpus* or *Rudraksha* and lived within the precincts of the temple. This was towards the end of the wordly career of Manikka Vacagar. He lived to compose a few more hymns, make a collection of all of them and give an authoritative exposition of them. At last he became absorbed in the image of his Maker at Chidambaram.

It will be seen from this sketch of the life of the saint that no mention is made of his visit to Malabar which was a part of the Chera kingdom. At the time we are speaking of, that kingdom was included in the Tamil land or *Tamilagam* as described in the *Tolkappiyam*, the oldest work extant on the science of Tamil literature. As there was free and constant communication between the three Tamil kingdoms Chera, Chola and Pandiya, Manikka Vacagar must have been familiar with all the sacred places there. Independently of this fact, a person who was anxious to pay his homage to God at the sacred shrines of the Chola and Pandiyan lands and the ancient Taprobane could not but have wished to visit the land of the Perumals with the same object. After relinquishing the office of Prime Minister at Madura, the only place of sanctity in the Pandiyan kingdom visited by Manikka Vacagar was Uttara Kosa Mangai—his favourite place of resort, though there were many others. The reason is not far to seek. He was born and brought up there, and subsequently directed its destinies. These circumstances must have given him the opportunity of visiting them before he laid down the seals of his office, and it is likely that he did not think it necessary to visit them over again. But as he had not visited all the places in the Chola country and Ceylon, he directed his footsteps towards those regions. In the same way, he must also have gone to Cheralam either during the period of his ministry or after its close. As far as we have been able to gauge, one of the objects of Manikka Vacagar in going to Ceylon was to confront the Buddhists who had overrun the island and convert them to his faith. Recognised Tamil works of antiquity and the researches of European *savants* of high repute show that Buddhism and Jainism were introduced into Malabar, which formed the major portion of the Chera kingdom, during the earlier period of the Christian era. The professors of the two religions were known to the Tamil speaking followers of the Caiva Siddhanta philosophy as *Chamaners.* It is likely that the Christians were also included in that category as the their religion flourished on that Coast side by side with Buddhism and Jainism. A person bent upon a mission of proselytism would naturaly have preferred a field nearer home for his labours, to a place situated beyond the seas. By this we do not mean to say that Manikka Vacagar did not visit Ceylon; all that we wish to impress upon our readers is, that he must have visited the kingdom of Chera before his advent to Ceylon. In the earlier portion of this paper we made mention of the imperfect and exaggerated view taken by the *Vâthavùr* puranam, and its unreliability as an historical work. Its silence on the visit of the saint to Malabar may be due to these causes. Again, the *Tiruvâcagam* itself is not explicit enough on the subject. When the sage passed on from shrine, to shrine as a rule he immortalised each in a hymn or more, but there are instances in which it does not appear that he dedicated any to some of the sacred places he visited. The Tamil sages, Jnana Sambandhar, Appar and Sundarar have sung of every sacred place they visited, and when the first and the third found it a difficult task to cross over to Ceylon to make their obeisance to God at the sacred places there, and sing of them, they posted themselves at Rameswaram on the opposite shore in Southern India, and proclaimed their sanctity. But all their hymns are not extant at present, and the fact is admitted on all hands. When such was the fate of the writings of the later-day saints, the works of Manikka Vacagar who is said to have flourished five or six centuries prior to their time must have shared a worse fate. It is generally supposed that he composed only fifty-one hymns, and that he himself published an authorised edition of the whole of them with the necessary annotations, before his death. For the reasons already stated, we are not prepared to accept this popular view. He must have certainly honoured every holy place he visited with his precious and sacred utterances.

We have already remarked that Manikka Vacagar was also anxious to save the souls of his fellow-men. In his perambulations he observed people—particularly women—making use of songs couched in indecent language both in connection with their spiritual and temporal affairs. He tried to reform them by putting into their mouths words capable of elevating their moral tone, and improving their devotional spirit. In the month of Margaly, corresponding to the *Tiruvathira* period in Malabar, it is usual for ladies in the Chola country, particulary at Tiru-Annamalai, to rise before dawn awake their slumbering sisters, bathe in the sacred waters, and attend Divine worship. The whole process is accompanied with songs. But as Manikka Vacagar was not pleased with those used by them at the time, he composed the *Tiruvempavai* or the maidens' song for such use. In the same way, he composed the *Tiru-port Sunnam* or "gold dust" to be sung when the temple women of Chidambaram pounded gold dust for the use of the God there. He also placed ladies of rank under obligations to him by composing a hymn to be sung during their pastime of *Ammanai* or the tossing of balls. A man like this who wanted to benefit himself and benefit others, would not have allowed opportunities to slip by without taking advantage of them to sing of God and His acts, and thus find balm to his much wearied soul. It may, therefore, be presumed that he must have sung in praise of every sacred place he visited, and that he must have visited all the holy shrines known at the time throughout the Tamil land including the kingdom of Chera. In case no hymn is forthcoming in honour of any known shrine, the inference is that it must have been lost.

With these observations we will now proceed to see if Manikka Vacagar did actually visit the Chera country. We have already referred to the King's commission to Manikka Vacagar to buy horses for his remount depot, on learning that a host of them had arrived from Arabia at the great sacred harbour, situated in the Chola country. This place is ordinarily called Avudaiyar Kovil, and according to tradition, the temple there which is noted for the exquisite beauty of its architecture, is said to have been built by the sage. But there is no *Turai*, (which means a port) anywhere near it, and the sea is about 15 or 20 miles from the place. There is also nothing to show that the sea washed Tiru-perum-turai and that it has since receded. We are therefore led to conclude that the geographical position of Tiru-perum-turai has, not been correctly given. From time immemorial there has been a more brisk trade between the Western Coast of Southern India and the regions beyond the Arabian Sea than between the latter and the Eastern Coast. For, the Western Coast is nearer to Arabia, Persia and other countries in Western Asia and Egypt, and the indentations on that Coast, afforded ready protection to ships that came to the shore after long and perilous voyages. Further, pepper, ivory, cardamom, peacocks, feathers, rice and ginger, the principal articles of export to Europe, were more easily procurable in the West Coast of India than anywhere else. Mariners sailing from the western countries of Asia and those bordering on them, were so thoroughly familiar with the ports on the Malabar Coast, that a merchantman with a cargo of horses from Arabia must naturally have discharged it there and there only.

There are also other grounds to arrive at this conclusion. The researches of eminent scholars show that the strip of land that lies between the sea and the lagoons in the Malabar Coast did not fully exist 1800 years ago, and that the sea washed the lands that lie on the eastern side of the lakes. According to Mr. Kanakasabhai Pillai, Trippunithura, the residence of His Highness the Rajah of Cochin, Kottayam and Kallada near Quilon must have once been seaports. Even granting that the narrow strips did exist 1800 years ago in their present dimensions, the several bars that communicate with the inland seas were deep enough to admit of the navigation of ships of ordinary size. The Cochin bar was one fo them, and we think the waters from it to Trippunithura were Navigable for Arab ships or *Pattimars.* Though Cochin and Cranganore had good roadsteads, merchants who were disposed to convey their commodities to the eastern side of the lagoons would have preferred to land them at Trippunithura to avoid a second transport across the inland sea. For, from early times there was communication through the Ghauts, between the Chera and the other two Tamil kingdoms. It was through these the ancestors of the Poonjat and Pandalam Royal families who were scions of the Pandiyan house entered Travancore. It was also through the same road that the heroine of the *Chilappathikaram*, one of the ancient Tamil classics, reached the banks of the Periyâr to yield up her gost. It is plain then, that commodities brought from Arabia and the countries about it could easily have been transported via Tiruppunithura to Madura, and to the Chola capital. For these reasons, we are of opinion that Trippunithura, the seat of His Highness the Rajah of Cochin, was Tiru-perum-turai the great sacred harbour referred to in the *Tiruvacagam* and the *Tiruvilaiyadal* puranam.

In addition to the grounds already urged and the similarity of names, there is internal evidence in Manikka Vacagar's great work, *the Tiruvacagam*, to prove that Trippunithura and Tiru-perum-turai are one and the same. In the second hymn which recites the glories of Civa, the sage delivers himself as follows:—

"In order that the world may be saved, the Lord of the bull came in grace with His Lady partner and bringing horses through the Kudanad he rode dexterously as a horseman." * According to Tamil authorities, the countries of Kuttam *i. e.*, Kuttanad and Kudam *i. e.*, Kodagu or Coorg were always under the sway of Chera, and on that ground his empire itself went by those names at times. The term *Kudam* also means west. The whole expression *Kudanad* thus means the western lands. The hymn was composed while Manikka Vacagar was at Chidambaram. Trippunithura lies to the west of that place as well as to the west

* *Tiruvacagam* 2nd Hymn, lines 25—29.

of Madura, from which Manikka Vacagar proceeded on his mission for the purchase of horses for the Pandiyan cavalry. It is then evident that he did not go towards the Eastern Coast to reach the great sacred harbour. His destination was the West Coast, and it was there he arranged for horses with the Arabs.

It will naturally be asked why Trippunithura on the West Coast close to Tiruvanjikalam—the western Chidambaram—is not regarded as sacred as the Tiru-perum-turai of the Eastern Coast by the Tamilians. About 1800 years ago the language of the West Coast of Southern India was undoubtedly Tamil, and the sacred places throughout the three kingdoms were the common property of all the people inhabiting them. But in course of time when they were divided by a difference in their dialects, their interests also became devided. This led to the gradual cessation of intercourse between them. Thus, most of the sacred shrines which have no Indian reputation, diminished in importance in the eyes of the inhabitants of the neighbouring kingdoms. Further, when certain holy places are unapproachable by the fact of their distance and other difficulties, some religious enthusiasts are supposed to have the permission of God to visit certain other places nearer home, and to derive the advantage of having visited the former. In this manner Manikka Vacagar might have made Tiru-perum-turai on the Eastern Coast, his favourite place of resort in after life; it may be mentioned here that one of the leading saints, Appar wanted to visit Kailas, but God is said to have ordered him to go to Tiruvâı ır five miles from Tanjore, on the promise of permitting him to reap the benefit of a pilgrimage to the seat of Civa himself on the Himalayas. In virtue of this convenient arrangement that place is now called *Dakshina-Kailas.* In like manner, many less notable saints appear to have enjoyed similar privileges. Again, there are other sacred places besides Tiru-perum-turai which bear the same name in the Chola and Chera countries and which have a common origin. By way of illustration, we may instance Kadavur and Tiruvalur. The correct name of the former which is situated in the Chola country is Tirukadaiyur, and is not far from Tanjore. It is noted for the sanctity of its cremation ground where Civa is said to have knocked down Yama, the God of death, while he attempted to seize Mârkandêya in the act of adoring him, and against His express wish. Almost the same scene is enacted annually at Kadavur, two miles from Quilon. Tiruvalore or more correctly Tiru-arur near Alwaye in Travancore, and the place which goes by the same name in the Tanjore District, have the same common origin in the valiant and pious acts of Emperor Masukunta of yore. We are not in a position to say which of such places are the original shrines and which their prototypes. When some of the scenes in the Mahabharata and Ramayana are laid in Malabar and particularly in Travancore and Cochin, we do not see why the prime source of sanctity of some of the Dravidian shrines should not be assigned to Malabar. Again, if we are to believe the account of the journey of Manikka Vacagar from Madura to Tiru-perum-turai as depicted in the *Vâthavûr* puranam, and of his having crossed jungles, hills and valleys, the scene must be laid in the "land of mountains".

There is still further evidence in support of this view. According to high Tamil authorities, Manikka Vacagar is said to have flourished about the beginning of the second century of the Christian era. This conclusion was arrived at by Mr. Tirumalai Kolundu Pillai of Coimbatore, and the late Mr. Suryanarayana Sastry of the Madras Christian College. Very recently, a writer in the Christian College Magazine fixed it a century later, confirming the view of Ittoop, a native writer of Travancore. On pages 84—85 of his work, Ittoop says:—

"About the year 270 A. D. a certain Manes who halied from Persia, and "who travelled all over China and other places in the far east, went to "Malabar and tried to influence the Christians there with his own peculiar "views, a mixture of Christianity and Buddhism."

He adds:—

"About the same time, a man who was named Manikka Vacagar, came "from the Chola country, practised sorcery, healed diseases of man and "beast by means of his incantations, instructed people in the use and, "efficacy of the sacred ashes, the five letters or *Panchakshharam* and *Panchakavyam*—the five products of the cow, and thus established a separate "community called the Manigramakars which was acknowledged by the "then reigning sovereign of Malabar—Veera Ragbava Perumal by dubbing "the leader of them as "the Loga Perum Chetty" or the greatest merchant "of the world."

The Rev. Mr. Whitehouse tells almost the same tale.* According to him the person said to have played the part referred to above, was either Manes the Persian, or Manikka Vacagar, the Caiva saint. He calls the five letters the "cabalistic sentences in verse." According to the historian Mosheim, Mr. Whitehouse says :—

"Eight families" were perverted by Manikka Vacagar and these so far "increased as to form at length a community of ninety-six houses whose "members had renounced the worship of the true God. The reigning Rajah "or Perumal Prince having granted to their headman, Iravi Corttan, ground "whereupon a settlement was formed called Manigramam, they were called "Manigramakars or (as we should say) the people of the village Manes and "the remnant of their descendants still bear the same name among the "Syrian Christians." (Page 47, Whitehouse).

Mr. Mackenzie extracts two passages confirming the version given above, but doubts the accuracy of the statements made therein.† Dr. Rae, late of the Madras Christian College, thinks that the story connected with the Manechians is a myth. Mr. Subramania Aiyar, the Census Commissioner of Travancore places the various theories before the public, but abstains from arriving at any definite conclusion.

We think it necessary to digress for a moment. There are writers like Dr. Rae who do not assign to Christianity in Malabar, the hoary age it has secured by the common consent of all. Dr. Rae is of opinion that Christianity must have been introduced into India by the Nestorians after the consolidation of their Church about the year 450 A. D. It appears that the first authentic account of a fully organised Church on the Malabar Coast was from the pen of Cosmas, an Alexandrian merchant, who visited the place about the year 522 A. D. To quote Dr. Rae, "The Church cannot have been

* Lingerings of Light in a Dark Land.

† Vol. III, The Madras Journal.

"of long standing, because the Persians, who from of old had "a horror of the sea, had just begun to develop a capacity and "a liking for navigation, and to work out schemes of com- "mercial aggrandisement."* These are negative proofs, and the Doctor does not positively say when Christianity was introduced into India. We think the following passages from Mr. Mackenzie's book and from the learned and well-digested Census Report of the state of Cochin by Mr. M. Sankara Menon will meet his arguments.

"All the Syrian Christians firmly believe that St. Thomas "landed at Cranganore in the year 52, established seven "churches on this Coast and suffered a martyr's death at "Mailapure or St. Thomas' Mount near the modern city of "Madras. This tradition was widely held from early times, "and it has been accepted as true by many writers of repute. "There is in the tradition itself nothing improbable. At that "date there was commerce between India and Europe by "caravans overland, by the Persian Gulf and by the Red sea, "so that the Apostle could journey to India."†

"We have of course no historical evidence for a positive conclusion, "and in the absence of any such, we have to look to circumstantial evidence "and balance the probabilities of the same. Viewed then with an unbiassed "mind, the early traditions, the extensive commercial intercourse that "existed between the East and the West, especially with the Malabar "Coast, much anterior to the Christian era, the testimony of the Holy "Fathers investigated and adverted to by Asseman, the continuity of "connection between the Malabar Church and the Eastern Patriarches and "Bishops from the very earliest times, and numberless references and "anecdotes by travellers, traders, historians and Churchmen,—all these tend "to make the apostolic origin of Christianity in Malabar highly probable. "Moreover, the unique success of the first mission lends additional colour "to this view. It is well known that the earliest converts to Christianity "on this coast were mostly from the higher orders of the Hindu society, and "included among them even Nambudris, the highest class of Malabar Hindus. "Considering the success of the mission in a region of Brahmin orthodoxy, "we may suppose it to have been possible only for a man of consummate wis- "dom, well versed in the gospel to present the new creed in a form attractive "to a highly religious and civilized people, and in those early times, none "but an Apostle of Christ, an eye-witness of his life and work, could have "been qualified for the work. The results of subsequent centuries tend "forcibly to illustrate the unique character of the first mission, for, while "the earliest converts were from the higher castes of the Malayali society,

* The Syrian Church in India, p. 116.

† Christianity in Travancore by Mr. G. T. Mackenzie, page 2.

"the labours of later missions have been fruitful almost entirely among the "lower orders." (Cochin Census Report, 1901, by Mr. M. Sankara Menon, "B. A., Part I, page 44).

It is not our object to pursue the subject further; Tradition should not be dubbed as "hoax and pious frauds" and "embellishments" meant to give greater sanctity to the religion of Christ, because they are traditions. There must be some substratum of truth in all of them, though there might be exaggerations. The differences of opinion noticed above do not go to nullify the theory that Manikka Vacagar visited Malabar. If some of the hypotheses put forward by Dr. Rae and others of his school are established, the utmost they can do is to bring the date of Manikka Vacagar nearer to ours; but we do not think that they have succeeded in proving their theories. It may therefore be presumed that the advent of St. Thomas to India took place about 52 A.D.

The introduction of the name of Manikka Vacagar into the works of writers on Christianity in Malabar does not stand alone as a mere statement uncorroborated by strong circumstantial evidence. Reference has already been made to some of them. We shall now try to obtain some side lights, and the first thing we would do is to trace the origin of the term Manigramam, which is of great archæological value and which contains a mine of information. We have seen that Manikka Vacagar occupied the proudest position of the first minister of a great potentate before he had completed his teens. In connection with his forced return to Madura from Tiru-perum-turai, we have seen that the tongue of jealousy was at work. There were not wanting people to carry tales against the young minister, and there were plausible circumstances against him. In reading between the lines, it seems that Manikka Vacagar was nicknamed *Mâni*, the Brahmin youth. The word *Mani* is Tamil and means an unmarried Brahmin youth or *Brahmachari*. It bears the same meaning in Canarese and Malayalam, but at present the word is confined to designate only Canarese or Tulu speaking Brahmin youths, or *Pottys* as they are called in this part of Southern India. The sage was originally known by the name of Vathavur, and when he was appointed the Prime Minister of the Pandiyan King he was named Tennavan Pirama Rayan. But since that date he must have been known as Mani amongst his subordinates and others to whom his appointment was distasteful. There are sufficient grounds to suppose that he went by the name of Manikka Vacagar towards the latter part of his career. When a person is initiated into the mysteries of the Caiva Siddhanta philosophy and renounces the world, it is usual for his *Guru* to call him by a new name. In addition to his other high qualifications Manikka Vacagar was a great *savant*. His culture in the Tamil and Sanskrit literatures was high and his learning was profound. But he was rather partial to his mother tongue, and he became distinguished for his pure diction and the melodious flow of his verses. As people became enamoured of his pious poetical compositions, they gradually changed the word Mani into *Manikkam* (ruby) and called him Manikka Vacagar, borrowing the sentiment from himself as found in the 26th stanza of the 5th hymn, *viz.*, "My mouth thou mad'st to speak abroad Thy *gem-like word*."* When therefore his *Guru* initiated him at Tiru-perum-turai, he gave him the name of Manikka Vacagar or "he of gem-like sentences," recognising the estimation in which he was held as a spiritual and moral teacher.

The term Manigramam then is derived from either Manes, the Persian, or, Manikka Vacagar, the Tamil saint. Here tradition is of immense value, and it is supported by existing circumstances. The Manechians were a heretic sect of Christians as we have already mentioned. Its founder regarded Christianity as incomplete and gave out that he was commissioned by God to perfect the system and lead its votaries to the Truth. Though Manes is said to have associated with the Buddhists of Central Asia during his travels in the far east and practised some of their austerities,

* Dr. Pope's translation of Tiru Vacagam.

still the system was a foreign one, and the difference between it and the Hindu faith was as wide as the poles; and the condition of the descendants of the Manigramakars who are found at present at Quilon, Kayancolam, Manor, Thiruvancode and other places in Travancore does not point to any connection with it. Though the Manigramakars do not own themselves as such, and try to screen themselves from being known as the descendants of a set of noble and heroic progenitors, still it is easy for any-body to spot the particular families in Travancore. They follow the Hindu faith, and are permitted to enter into all sacred places. In fact, they enjoy almost all the privileges of ordinary Nairs. But, in the case of inter-dining and intermarriages, there is not that freedom, though the reluctance on the part of those who have stood steadfast to their ancestral faith is fast dying out. The following quotation may with advantage be made respecting their present condition.

> "These unhappy people are not at their ease even among their new "friends; they have not found all their carnal hearts wanted, and God grant "they never may; so that, after feeding on husks, they may be brought to "consider their ways, and turn unto Him whom their forefathers forsook! "Though most of them occupy a respectable position—being very commonly "employed about the local courts; and though they intermarry with Nair, "and even Brahmin families, they are looked down upon by the people of "their choise. Thus, if a Nair makes a feast, the males of the Manigramakar "may be invited, but not the females; and if they make a feast in return, "the Nair guests will not eat the food if cooked by any one of the same caste "as their host. When the Nairs and they fall out, it is a very common thing "for the former to upbraid them with their mongrel origin." (Lingerings of Light in a Dark Land, page 50.)

It may be doubted whether Hinduism received back into its fold its misdirected sons. That the practice was prevalent in the Tamil land, if not elsewhere, can be abundantly proved. The *Vathavur* Puranam refers to such reconversions from Buddhism. Tirunâvukarasu or Appar who was born and brought up in orthodox Caivism, went to Patalipuram, a seat of learning and the headquarters of Jainism. There he learned its system, and convinced that it was the only true religion, became a convert to it and finally the chief priest of that religion. But owing to subsequent conviction he relapsed into Caiva Siddhantism and was received with open arms by its followers. He afterwards became a teacher in that particular faith, and his memory is held in great reverence by the followers of Caiva Siddhanta philosophy. Our readers must have heard how Jnana Sambandhar became victorious in a disputation between himself and the Jains in the presence of the ruling Pandiyan at Madura, how some of the discomfited Jains were reconverted to Caiva faith and how the rest were sent to the gallows. Thus, under the Caiva Siddhanta which owes its origin to the combined efforts of the Aryans and the Dravidians, there is not the least objection to proselytism.

It is an historical fact that in a *Sasanam* or charter granted in the year 774 by the then Cheraman Perumal, particular mention is made of the Manigramakars along with the Jews. I believe that a special concession was granted to a small but rising community, and according to some writers the then rulers of the country encouraged them in their apostacy. These facts go to show that the charter was not granted to the Christians. Mr. Whitehouse speaks of thirty families of Manigramakars at Quilon and their priest who went by the name of *Naimar*. It seems that he had a subordinate officer who went by the name of *Veera Udayan* armed with a weapon called *Yamadhuda*, and his duty was to collect the dues from the low class artisans. Mr. Whitehouse adds that the Manigramakars maintained only a remote connection with the Christian Church and that they were desirous of being treated on a footing of equality with their Hindu brethren.* In this account there seems to be some reference to a temple dedicated to Badrakali in the vicinity of Quilon, but for fear of wounding the feelings of some of its principal votaries, and office-bearers, we refrain from referring to them more specifically. From these facts we can confidently conclude that the class of Manigramakars do exist at present in Travancore, and likely at Cochin, the place of its origin, that they are descendants of reconverts from Christianity, that they follow the Hindu faith at present, and that they have been named after Manikka Vacagar, the Caiva saint.

* Vide Lingerings of light in a Dark Land, Page, 49.

The legend of the metamorphosis of the foxes of the jungles into well-broken stately steeds bears testimony to the reconversion of the apostate Hindus. The exclusive-Aryan religion has not been encouraging proselytism, much less the readmission of its weakminded sons into its fold. The system of reconversion, as has already been stated, is a purely Dravidian institution and it has always been looked down upon by the Aryans. A story that is current in the Tamil country graphically describes the attitude of its opponents. A certain Sudra who basked in the sunshine of royal favour was requested by his King to name his reward for his fidelity. In response, the favourite said that he wished to be made a Brahmin. The King agreed and ordered the necessary ceremonies to be gone through at the river side to bring about the second birth of the man. When the priests were busily engaged, Thennal Raman, the court jester, carried a jet blâck dog to the neighbourhood, held it by its legs, and went on striking it hard against a stone which was lying there for the purpose of bleaching clothes. The assembled priests heard the piteous shrieks of the dog, ran up to Thennal Raman and interrogated him with regard to his inhuman act. In reply he said that he was engaged in converting a jet black dog into a snow white one. An idea like this must have been working in the minds of Brahmins when Manikka Vacagar–an out and out Dravidian in spirit,—was endeavouring to bring back the Christians of Malabar to their ancestral faith, and they must have given vent to their feelings by giving out that he wanted to convert foxes into horses. As time went on, the statement must have been handed down from generation to generation till it came to be believed as true and found a place in two of the Puranams of the Dravidians.

From a traditionary account related by Mr. Whitehouse* it seems that the labours of Manikka Vacagar extended as far as Cape Comorin. In the north they began at Malankara close to Cranganore.

* See page 74.

To conclude, it will be seen from the foregoing that the saint did visit the Malabar Coast, and carried on his labours of proselytism amongst the native Christians of the Syrian church, in such an aggressive form, as to call forth the wrath of the ministers of that religious denomination. Their reference to his practice of Sorcery, healing of diseases by means of incantations, his instructions in the use and efficacy of the sacred ashes, the five sacramental letters, and the five products of the cow, unmistakably point to him and to him alone, as the disturber of peace, amongst the members of their flock and he could therefore in no way be mistaken for Manes, the Central Asian pilgrim. For, the latter could not have dealt with certain symbolisms and practices which were peculiar to Hinduism. Further, Manikka Vacagar, the greatest opponent of the religions of the Chamanars of the age could not have preached the tenets of Buddhism, coupled with those of Christian gospel, as said to have been done by Manes. In the next place it was not possible for the Central Asian traveller, to have bequeathed an imperishable monument of his labour in the class of Manigramakars, who are essentially Hindus in habit, faith and thought. In these circumstances any pronouncement made while under the influence of *Odium Theologicum* favour of an opponent must unconditionally be accepted as true. The antiquity assigned therefore to Manikka Vacagar by the Christians, who cherished no feelings of love for him, can in no way be an exaggeration and when they refer to certain incidents of the year 270 A. D. connecting his name, the date should be considered with all seriousness. It can be therefore safely be considered that he was engaged in that year in Malabar in the work of active proselytism, of which there is ample testimony in the Tiru Vacagam.

In addition to the evidence, that has been set forth to establish the visit of Manikka Vacagar to Malabar it may be mentioned that the diction employed in the Tiru Vacagam goes to confirm the fact. Though a language that is spoken and written in different parts of a country may be pure, every locality has its own peculiarities. The Malayalam is an offshoot of the Tamil and the manner in which the former differentiates herself from the latter, is by the maintenance of peculiar use of words and expressions belonging to it and it pervades the whole of Tiru Vacagam. Two of the ancient classics Chilappathikaram and Manimêkalai are undoubted productions of the Malabar Coast and they in common with Tiru Vacagaṁ contain a large number of words and expressions which are ordinarily used in Malayalam but are of re-occurrence in other Tamil classics or the present day Tamil. The similarity of diction that runs through the three works, go to show that they belong to one and the same age and locality. With regard to the last, it may be mentioned that a long sojourn on the part of Manikka Vacagar in a country which was to give birth to the Malayalam language may have tainted his tongue and unconsciously induced him to imbibe the provincialisms. This question also enables us to determine the age of Manikka Vacagar. In discussing the period of Chilappathikaram and Manimêkalai elsewhere I have assigned the beginning of the second century, and others working in the same field as I do, have held the same view. On the ground of affinity that exists between the TiruVacagam and the two classics their age may be given to it.

However the weight of evidence does not go beyond the third century; thus the time of Manikka Vacagar may be put down between the 2nd and 3rd centuries of the Christian era.